my **revision** notes

Pearson Edexcel A-level

POLITICS
GLOBAL POLITICS

John Jefferies

HODDER EDUCATION
AN HACHETTE UK COMPANY

Acknowledgements
Every effort has been made to trace all copyright holders, but if any have been inadvertently overlooked, the Publishers will be pleased to make the necessary arrangements at the first opportunity.

Orders: please contact Bookpoint Ltd, 130 Park Drive, Milton Park, Abingdon, Oxon OX14 4SE. Telephone: (44) 01235 827827. Fax: (44) 01235 400401. Email education@bookpoint.co.uk Lines are open from 9 a.m. to 5 p.m., Monday to Saturday, with a 24-hour message answering service. You can also order through our website: www.hoddereducation.co.uk

ISBN: 978 1 5104 7172 6

First published in 2020 by

Hodder Education,

An Hachette UK Company

Carmelite House

50 Victoria Embankment

London EC4Y 0DZ

www.hoddereducation.co.uk

Impression number 10 9 8 7 6 5 4 3 2 1

Year 2024 2023 2022 2021 2020

Typeset by Integra Software Services Pvt. Ltd., Pondicherry, India

Printed in Spain

A catalogue record for this title is available from the British Library.

Get the most from this book

Everyone has to decide his or her own revision strategy, but it is essential to review your work, learn it and test your understanding. These Revision Notes will help you to do that in a planned way, topic by topic. Use this book as the cornerstone of your revision and don't hesitate to write in it — personalise your notes and check your progress by ticking off each section as you revise.

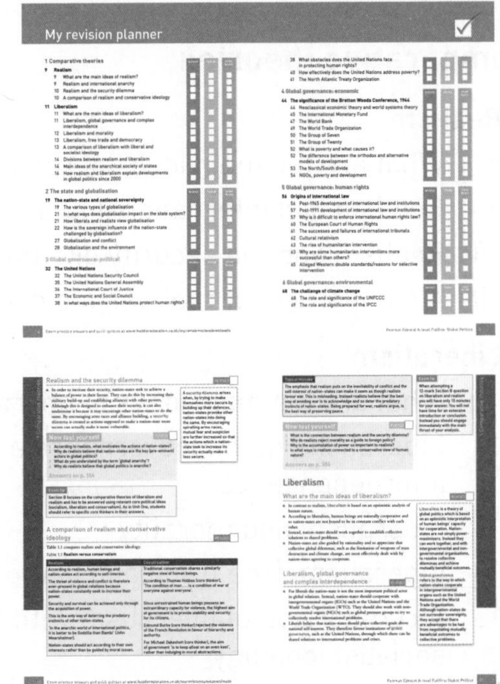

Tick to track your progress

Use the revision planner on pages 4 to 7 to plan your revision, topic by topic. Tick each box when you have:

- revised and understood a topic
- tested yourself
- practised the exam questions and gone online to check your answers and complete the quick quizzes

You can also keep track of your revision by ticking off each topic heading in the book. You may find it helpful to add your own notes as you work through each topic.

Features to help you succeed

Exam tips

Expert tips are given throughout the book to help you polish your exam technique in order to maximise your chances in the exam.

Typical mistakes

The author identifies the typical mistakes candidates make and explains how you can avoid them.

Now test yourself

These short, knowledge-based questions provide the first step in testing your learning. Answers are at the back of the book.

Definitions and key words

Clear, concise definitions of essential key terms are provided where they first appear.

Key words from the specification are highlighted in bold throughout the book.

Debates

Debates are highlighted to help you assess arguments and use evidence appropriately.

Exam practice

Practice exam questions are provided for each topic. Use them to consolidate your revision and practise your exam skills.

Summaries

The summaries provide a quick-check bullet list for each topic.

Online

Go online to check your answers to the exam questions and try out the extra quick quizzes at **www.hoddereducation.co.uk/myrevisionnotesdownloads**

My revision planner

1 Comparative theories

REVISED TESTED EXAM READY

2 The state and globalisation

REVISED TESTED EXAM READY

3 Global governance: political

REVISED TESTED EXAM READY

4 Global governance: economic

REVISED | TESTED | EXAM READY

5 Global governance: human rights

6 Global governance: environmental

REVISED | TESTED | EXAM READY

7 Power and developments

REVISED TESTED EXAM READY

8 Regionalism and the European Union

REVISED TESTED EXAM READY

Countdown to my exams

6–8 weeks to go

- Start by looking at the specification — make sure you know exactly what material you need to revise and the style of the examination. Use the revision planner on pages 4 to 7 to familiarise yourself with the topics.
- Organise your notes, making sure you have covered everything on the specification. The revision planner will help you to group your notes into topics.
- Work out a realistic revision plan that will allow you time for relaxation. Set aside days and times for all the subjects that you need to study, and stick to your timetable.
- Set yourself sensible targets. Break your revision down into focused sessions of around 40 minutes, divided by breaks. These Revision Notes organise the basic facts into short, memorable sections to make revising easier.

REVISED ☐

2–6 weeks to go

- Read through the relevant sections of this book and refer to the exam tips, exam summaries, typical mistakes and key terms. Tick off the topics as you feel confident about them. Highlight those topics you find difficult and look at them again in detail.
- Test your understanding of each topic by working through the 'Now test yourself' questions in the book. Look up the answers at the back of the book.
- Make a note of any problem areas as you revise, and ask your teacher to go over these in class.
- Look at past papers. They are one of the best ways to revise and practise your exam skills. Write or prepare planned answers to the exam practice questions provided in this book. Check your answers online and try out the extra quick quizzes at **www.hoddereducation.co.uk/myrevisionnotesdownloads**
- Use the revision activities to try out different revision methods. For example, you can make notes using mind maps, spider diagrams or flash cards.
- Track your progress using the revision planner and give yourself a reward when you have achieved your target.

REVISED ☐

One week to go

- Try to fit in at least one more timed practice of an entire past paper and seek feedback from your teacher, comparing your work closely with the mark scheme.
- Check the revision planner to make sure you haven't missed out any topics. Brush up on any areas of difficulty by talking them over with a friend or getting help from your teacher.
- Attend any revision classes put on by your teacher. Remember, he or she is an expert at preparing people for examinations.

REVISED ☐

The day before the examination

- Flick through these Revision Notes for useful reminders, for example the exam tips, exam summaries, typical mistakes and key terms.
- Check the time and place of your examination.
- Make sure you have everything you need — extra pens and pencils, tissues, a watch, bottled water, sweets.
- Allow some time to relax and have an early night to ensure you are fresh and alert for the examinations.

REVISED ☐

My exams

A-level Politics Paper 1

Date:...

Time:...

Location:..

A-level Politics Paper 2

Date:...

Time:...

Location:..

1 Comparative theories

Realism

What are the main ideas of realism?

REVISED

- Classical **realism** provides a negative interpretation of human nature. Human beings are self-seeking, selfish and egotistical and so constantly strive for their own advantage.
- Niccolò Machiavelli in *The Prince* (1513) states that human beings are 'insatiable, arrogant, crafty and shifting, and above all malignant, iniquitous, violent and savage'.
- According to structural realism, nation-states, like human beings, seek to advance their own interests at the expense of other nation-states.
- Nation-states are power-maximisers which constantly seek the best outcomes for themselves.
- The nation-state is also sovereign, which means that it possesses absolute authority to act according to its own best interests.
- Since there is no authority greater than the nation-state, the nation-state is the key actor in global politics. The nation-state cannot rely on institutions of global governance, such as the United Nations (UN), to protect its security.
- The 'billiard ball model' of global relations can be used to represent the centrality of state sovereignty in realist political theory. This is because all nation-states are equally sovereign and, like the hard shell of billiard balls, their sovereignty is protected from outside forces.

Realism is a theory of global politics which regards nation-states as the central actors in international relations. Since nation-states pursue self-interest, and there is no authority greater than the nation-state that can enforce stability, this means that international relations tend towards conflict.

Exam tip

Realism and liberalism are theories of global politics which provide two contrasting interpretations of international relations. These two conflicting perspectives of international relations are specifically examined in a compulsory 12-mark question in Section B, although they should also be applied *throughout* the exam.

Realism and international anarchy

REVISED

- Since nation-states are sovereign and relentlessly pursue their own self-interest, they will not accept a supranational authority greater than themselves. As a result, global relations are anarchic because there is no authority which can effectively enforce international laws to which all states are equally accountable.
- Nation-states exist in a 'self-help' world since, according to the realist political philosopher John Mearsheimer, there is no 'night watchman' that can enforce rules of international behaviour.
- The state of **international anarchy** does not mean that war is inevitable. However, there is always the *threat* of war as nation-states constantly seek to increase their power and security.
- According to the Greek historian Thucydides (460 BCE–400 BCE), 'Peace is an armistice in a war that is continually going on'.
- In order to survive in such a hostile world order, nation-states need to maximise their own security.
- States should not act according to moral or humanitarian impulses since this is likely to destabilise international relations.
- The five key words associated with realism are:
  - state
  - security
  - self-help
  - sovereignty
  - survival.

International anarchy means that since, according to realism, there is no authority greater than the nation-state that can compel obedience global relations are anarchic. As a result, nation-states must protect themselves from other nation-states rather than relying on any superior law-enforcing body to do this for them.

Realism and the security dilemma

REVISED

- In order to increase their security, nation-states seek to achieve a balance of power in their favour. They can do this by increasing their military build-up and establishing alliances with other powers.
- Although this is designed to enhance their security, it can also undermine it because it may encourage other nation-states to do the same. By encouraging arms races and alliance building, a **security dilemma** is created as actions supposed to make a nation-state more secure can actually make it more vulnerable.

A **security dilemma** arises when, by trying to make themselves more secure by building up their defences, nation-states provoke other nation-states into doing the same. By encouraging spiralling arms races, mutual fear and suspicion are further increased so that the actions which a nation-state took to increase its security actually make it less secure.

Now test yourself

TESTED

1 According to realists, what motivates the actions of nation-states?
2 Why do realists believe that nation-states are the key (pre-eminent) actors in global politics?
3 What do you understand by the term 'global anarchy'?
4 Why do realists believe that global politics is anarchic?

Answers on p. 106

Exam tip

Section B focuses on the comparative theories of liberalism and realism and *has* to be answered using relevant core political ideas (socialism, liberalism and conservatism). As in Unit One, students should refer to specific core thinkers in their answers.

A comparison of realism and conservative ideology

REVISED

Table 1.1 compares realism and conservative ideology.

Table 1.1 Realism versus conservatism

Realism	Conservatism
According to realism, human beings and nation-states act according to self-interest.	Traditional conservatism shares a similarly negative view of human beings.
The threat of violence and conflict is therefore ever-present in global relations because nation-states constantly seek to increase their power.	According to Thomas Hobbes (core thinker), 'The condition of man . . . is a condition of war of everyone against everyone'.
Security and survival can be achieved only through the acquisition of power. This is the only way of deterring the predatory instincts of other nation-states.	Since unrestrained human beings possess an extraordinary capacity for violence, the highest aim of government is to provide stability and security for its citizens.
'In the anarchic world of international politics, it is better to be Godzilla than Bambi' (John Mearsheimer).	Edmund Burke (core thinker) rejected the violence of the French Revolution in favour of hierarchy and authority.
Nation-states should act according to their own interests rather than be guided by moral issues.	For Michael Oakeshott (core thinker), the aim of government 'is to keep afloat on an even keel', rather than indulging in moral abstractions.

Typical mistake

The emphasis that realism puts on the inevitability of conflict and the self-interest of nation-states can make it seem as though realists favour war. This is misleading. Instead realists believe that the best way of avoiding war is to acknowledge and so deter the predatory instincts of nation-states. Being prepared for war, realists argue, is the best way of preserving peace.

Exam tip

When attempting a 12-mark Section B question on liberalism and realism you will have only 15 minutes for your answer. You will not have time for an extensive introduction or conclusion. Instead you should engage immediately with the main thrust of your analysis.

Now test yourself

TESTED

5 What is the connection between realism and the security dilemma?
6 Why do realists reject morality as a guide to foreign policy?
7 Why is the accumulation of power so important to realists?
8 In what ways is realism connected to a conservative view of human nature?

Answers on p. 106

Liberalism

What are the main ideas of liberalism?

REVISED

- In contrast to realism, **liberalism** is based on an optimistic analysis of human nature.
- According to liberalism, human beings are naturally cooperative and so nation-states are not bound to be in constant conflict with each other.
- Instead, nation-states should work together to establish collective solutions to shared problems.
- Nation-states are also guided by rationality and so appreciate that collective global dilemmas, such as the limitation of weapons of mass destruction and climate change, are most effectively dealt with by nation-states agreeing to cooperate.

Liberalism is a theory of global politics which is based on an optimistic interpretation of human beings' capacity for cooperation. Nation-states are not simply power-maximisers. Instead they can work together, and with intergovernmental and non-governmental organisations, to resolve collective dilemmas and achieve mutually beneficial outcomes.

Global governance refers to the way in which nation-states cooperate in intergovernmental organs such as the United Nations and the World Trade Organization. Although nation-states do not surrender sovereignty, they accept that there are advantages to be had from negotiating mutually beneficial outcomes to collective problems.

Liberalism, global governance and complex interdependence

REVISED

- For liberals the nation-state is not the most important political actor in global relations. Instead, nation-states should cooperate with intergovernmental organs (IGOs) such as the United Nations and the World Trade Organization (WTO). They should also work with non-governmental organs (NGOs) such as global pressure groups to try to collectively resolve international problems.
- Liberals believe that nation-states should place collective goals above national self-interest. They therefore favour institutions of **global governance**, such as the United Nations, through which there can be shared solutions to international problems and crises.

- The way in which nation-states work with each other and with NGOs and IGOs creates a world of **complex interdependence** based on multiple channels of communication.
- This creates a 'cobweb model' of international relations which brings together nation-states, IGOs and NGOs in mutually supporting layers of connectivity.
- According to liberals, international relations can be based on harmony and balance because nation-states can rationally decide that they can achieve more through collective action rather than through national self-interest. War and conflict are not inevitable in international relations.
- By accepting practical limitations on their sovereignty through their membership of intergovernmental organs, the foundations can be established for **world government**. This would be based on the complete abandonment of state egoism in favour of a shared approach to international decision-making.

Complex interdependence is a theory central to liberalism suggesting that the interests of nation-states are closely connected through a multitude of interactions. Diverse channels of communication create a cobweb model of interconnectedness based on mutually beneficial outcomes, which challenges state egoism as the key influence in international relations.

World government would be one that possessed legitimate executive and legislative sovereignty. It would establish a supranational authority to which all nation-states would be accountable.

Liberalism and morality

REVISED

- Liberalism is also founded on a moral interpretation of global politics which emphasises the importance of the protection of human rights when determining foreign policy.
- Since liberals argue that the world is a global community based on our common humanity, nation-states have a duty to protect and encourage international respect for human rights.
- A good example of this is the UN's Responsibility to Protect (2005), which recognises that a nation-state has the 'responsibility' to protect the human rights of its citizens. The global community in turn has the 'responsibility' to intervene in the internal affairs of a nation-state if those rights are being abused.
- The liberal belief in our shared humanity has been used to justify humanitarian interventions within sovereign nation-states, including the NATO interventions in Kosovo (1999) and Libya (2011).

Liberalism, free trade and democracy

REVISED

- According to the principles of liberalism, democracies do not go to war with each other. Liberals encourage the spread of democracy in order to encourage global peace and stability. This is often referred to as the democratic peace thesis.
- Liberals believe that free trade is both an economic and a moral good. This is because trade between nation-states encourages cooperation and understanding and so reduces the risk of war.
- Liberals support the extension of free trade and democracy as the most effective way of encouraging cooperation in order to increase *zones of peace* at the expense of *zones of conflict*.

Typical mistake

Although liberalism as a theory of global politics is closely connected with the core ideology of liberalism, its optimistic interpretation of human nature also owes a great deal to socialism. Therefore, when answering a Section B question on liberalism, be prepared to connect it to both the core theories of liberalism and socialism.

Now test yourself

TESTED

9 How do liberals view human nature? Why is this significant in the way in which they approach international relations?
10 What is global governance and why do liberals favour it?
11 In what way and why is the protection of human rights important to liberals?
12 Why do liberals believe that democracy and free trade are important?

Answers on p. 106

A comparison of liberalism with liberal and socialist ideology

REVISED

Table 1.2 compares liberalism with liberal and socialist ideology.

Table 1.2 Liberalism versus liberal and socialist ideology

Liberalism	Liberal and socialist ideology
Liberalism's optimistic interpretation of human nature suggests that global relations can be defined by harmony and balance. War and conflict are therefore not inevitable in global relations. Nation-states should work together, and with IGOs and NGOs, in order to resolve collective problems. Nation-states should act according to shared goals to encourage the establishment of a global community. Nation-states achieve more through cooperating with each other than by competing. Collective interdependence is the most effective way of encouraging peace and stability. Morality ought to provide a basis for global decision-making. Human rights protection therefore ought to play a key role in international decision-making.	Liberal optimism about the possibility of universal peace and harmony is closely associated with the positive socialist view of human nature. According to Marx and Engels (core socialist thinkers), human beings are naturally communal and achieve most when they cooperate rather than compete. John Locke (core liberal thinker) argues that human beings are rational and so enter into social contracts since they appreciate that they achieve most by agreeing to be governed according to the rule of law. The liberal belief in the collective advantages created through the establishment of institutions of global governance is closely connected with Locke's political philosophy. Mary Wollstonecraft and Betty Friedan (core liberal thinkers) emphasise the importance of equal rights, which underpins a moral approach to foreign policy.

Divisions between realism and liberalism

REVISED

Table 1.3 looks at the divisions between liberalism and realism.

Table 1.3 Liberalism versus realism

Realism	Liberalism
According to classical realism, human beings relentlessly seek power and so the relationship between nation-states will always be conflict-based.	Liberalism derives from a much more optimistic interpretation of human nature. Human beings are naturally cooperative and rational.
Structural realism focuses on the way in which nation-states are sovereign and independent and so do not have to accept the authority of any higher supranational body. Since nation-states are not accountable to any superior body, global relations are anarchic.	They can therefore appreciate the mutually beneficial outcomes to be had from pursuing collective responses to collective dilemmas. Liberals reject the realist view that the self-interest of the nation-state (state egoism) is the core motivating factor in global politics.
Realists reject attempts to limit the power of the nation-state and are sceptical about institutions of global governance such as the United Nations.	Instead, liberals argue that nation-states are only one of many actors in international relations.
The centrality of nation-states in global politics means that there is always the potential for conflict because nation-states are 'power-maximisers' and there is no superior body that can intervene to enforce stability.	Nation-states should therefore cooperate with each other in intergovernmental organs such as the United Nations and work with non-governmental organs, such as global pressure groups, to try to resolve collective dilemmas.
Nation-states exist in a 'self-help' world and so protect their security by establishing favourable alliances and building up their defences.	Liberals believe in an approach to global politics in which cooperation provides favourable outcomes for all involved.
Unfortunately, by building up diplomatic and military influence in order to protect themselves, nation-states can make other nation-states feel vulnerable and so this encourages them to do the same. This can spiral into a security dilemma since attempts to make a nation-state more secure may make it less secure by encouraging destabilising arms races.	Liberals favour the development of global governance since the more that nation-states cooperate, the more state egoism is challenged. This will create such a complex web of **interconnectedness** that the harmful rivalry of nation-states will be merged in a shared pursuit of collective interests.
The extent to which human rights are protected is purely an issue for nation-states.	The protection of human rights must be of central importance in international relations.

Interconnectedness means that as a result of globalisation, nation-states have become so interlinked that it has led to a cobweb state of mutual dependence.

Main ideas of the anarchical society of states

REVISED

In 1977 the political scientist Hedley Bull published *The Anarchical Society*.

- Bull argued that although nation-states still play the dominant role in international relations, this does not mean that there must therefore be constant war and conflict.
- This is because nation-states, although they are still sovereign, choose to cooperate with other nation-states to achieve positive outcomes for themselves.

- Global politics is still anarchic because there is no supranational body that can compel obedience. However, there are still numerous channels through which nation-states can choose to cooperate rather than compete.
- As a result, it is possible to create order and stability out of global anarchy. By seeing mutual advantages in cooperation, a society (rather than just a system) of states is created.
- It is possible for there to be an **anarchical society of states**. This is because although sovereign nation-states remain the key actors in global politics, they generally choose to act according to accepted rules of international behaviour and abide by international law.
- Anarchical society theory attempts to bridge the gap between realist and liberal interpretations of global politics.
- By accepting the nation-state as the key actor in global relations, anarchical society is within the realist tradition. However, by arguing that nation-states generally choose to cooperate, it challenges the realist emphasis on state egoism, placing it within a more liberal interpretation of international relations.

Anarchical society of states is a term associated with Hedley Bull and the English School of political philosophy. Bull accepts that nation-states are the central actors in global politics. However, he argues that they can choose to cooperate with each other in order to achieve mutually beneficial outcomes. This therefore creates a global society *in spite of* the anarchical nature of the international system.

Exam tip

You will impress the examiner if you are able to support your analysis of realism and liberalism with contemporary examples in practice. For example, you could argue that the Trump administration's opposition to the International Criminal Court (ICC) is an example of realism. Regional organisations, such as the European Union (EU), which are based on the pooling of sovereignty, provide a good example of the practical implementation of liberalism.

Francis Fukuyama's *The End of History and the Last Man* and Samuel Huntington's *The Clash of Civilizations* provide two contrasting interpretations of the way in which global relations could develop in the twenty-first century (see Table 1.4).

Table 1.4 Fukuyama and Huntington: a comparison

Francis Fukuyama, *The End of History* (1992)	Samuel Huntington, *The Clash of Civilizations* (1996)
Francis Fukuyama wrote *The End of History and the Last Man* at the end of the Cold War. According to Fukuyama, the collapse of the Soviet Union indicated that liberal democracy and free trade would become the dominant force in global relations. As a result, ideological conflicts would gradually be replaced by the global acceptance of liberal democracy. According to Karl Marx, 'the end of history' would be communism. However, for Fukuyama, the 'end of history' will be 'the universalization of Western liberal democracy as the final form of human government'. The globalisation of liberal democracy will create a new global stability based on shared values and mutual interdependence.	Huntington's *The Clash of Civilizations and the Remaking of the World Order* is based on a more realist approach to global politics. According to Huntington, international relations will always be based on conflict. This is because there is a continual struggle for power and influence. However, the nation-state is not central to Huntington's theory of global politics. This distinguishes him from mainstream realism. Instead, Huntington argues that conflict in the post-Cold War world will be caused by the rivalry of different civilisations. Controversially, Huntington argues that the dominant rivalry is between Islamic civilisation and Western liberal civilisation. According to Huntington, these civilisations will clash because their values cannot be reconciled.

How realism and liberalism explain developments in global politics since 2000

REVISED

Liberalism

- The end of the Cold War (c.1989–1991) encouraged the development of a more liberal world order. It was within this context that Fukuyama envisaged *The End of History*.
- In 1991 a global coalition, led by the United States but mandated by the United Nations, was established to expel Iraqi forces from Kuwait. This suggests that a liberal world order based on shared respect for international law is possible.
- The setting up of UN tribunals (former Yugoslavia, Cambodia, Sierra and Rwanda) and the creation of the International Criminal Court in 2002 indicated that human rights would now play a more central role in international relations.
- The UN World Summit which endorsed the UN Responsibility to Protect (2005) established the important liberal principle that nation-states have a duty to protect the human rights of people living within their borders.
- The way in which World Bank and International Monetary Fund (IMF) structural adjustment programmes have driven forward liberal economic principles suggests that the free-market/free-trade principles of **the Washington Consensus** are becoming globally dominant.
- The establishment of the North American Free Trade Agreement (NAFTA) in 1994 further demonstrated the growing importance of free trade between nation-states.
- The expansion and further integration of the European Union provides a liberal global template for how nation-states can agree to share sovereignty in order to maximise their collective good.
- The growing scope of climate change agreements (Rio de Janeiro, Kyoto, Copenhagen and Paris) demonstrates how nation-states can be willing to work together to resolve collective dilemmas.

The Washington Consensus is another term for economic liberalism. Liberalism is closely associated with the expansion of free markets and free trade. It means that nation-states should *not* protect themselves from foreign competition with excessive tariffs and subsidies to their own industries.

Realism

- Nation-states often continue to be motivated by realist principles. Indeed, realist self-interest has become even more important recently as strongly nationalist governments increasingly put their national interests before those of the global community.
- In 2014, Russia annexed Crimea from Ukraine in order to advance its national interests in defiance of international law.
- The Trump administration withdrew from the Paris Treaty in 2017 because fulfilling the terms of the agreement was not in the United States' immediate economic interests.
- President Trump has stated 'we reject globalism' in favour of the national interest. In his inaugural speech (2017), he explicitly rejected liberalism when he stated, 'It is the right of all nations to put their own interests first'.
- The international community has not been able to come together to resolve humanitarian crises in Syria and Yemen because nation-states have preferred to put their strategic interests first.

- For example, Russia and Iran have intervened in Syria in order to advance their geostrategic interests. Saudi Arabia has intervened in Yemen to stop Shia rebels toppling the government which would be likely to increase Iranian influence in the region.
- China is advancing its territorial interests in the South China Sea by reef building. Although China's claim to the Spratly Islands has been declared illegal by an international tribunal, China has ignored the ruling.
- Although the European Union is widely seen as being the world's most advanced form of liberal-inspired regionalism, it is now being challenged by the rise of nationalist/populist political parties.
- The popularity of the nationalist principles of Viktor Orbán in Hungary and Matteo Salvini in Iraly strongly contrasts with the liberal principles on which the EEC/EU was established.
- The way in which the Paris Treaty (2015) is based on nation-states submitting their own carbon-reduction targets (Intended Determined National Contributions) shows how unwilling nation-states still are to accept limitations on their sovereignty.
- The growing assertiveness of China and Russia is likely to further challenge liberal values since both are strongly Westphalian and put their geostrategic interests ahead of a liberal commitment to human rights.
- The extent to which global politics reflects liberalism is less marked than it was in the immediate aftermath of the Cold War.

Exam tip

In 1648, the Peace of Westphalia ended the Thirty Years War (1618–1648) by applying the principle that nation-states could not claim the right to interfere within the internal affairs of other nation-states. The phrase 'Westphalian principles' is therefore often used by realists to explain the sovereign right of nation-states to exercise exclusive power within their own borders.

Exam practice

The section B question on **comparative theories** is **compulsory** and is worth 12 marks. It will always begin with the word 'Analyse'.

Six marks will be awarded for knowledge (AO1) and six marks will be awarded for analysis (AO2).

The question will always include the phrase, 'In your answer you must discuss any relevant core political ideas'. This means that students will have to refer to conservative, socialist and/or liberal core theory and theorists in their responses.

1 Analyse the divisions in relation to human nature which exist between realists and liberals. In your answer you must discuss any relevant core political ideas. [12]
2 Analyse the meaning and significance of the anarchical society theory. In your answer you must discuss any relevant core political ideas. [12]
3 Analyse the reasons why realists and liberals view the role of the nation-state in global politics so differently. In your answer you must discuss any relevant core political ideas. [12]
4 Analyse the reasons why realists and liberals view the acquisition of power in international relations in different ways. In your answer you must discuss any relevant core political ideas. [12]

Answers and quick quiz 1 online

ONLINE

Summary

You should now have an understanding of the following:

- the significance of the different ways in which realists and liberals understand human nature
- why realists regard the acquisition of power as so important in global politics
- the significance of the security dilemma
- the meaning of complex interdependence and why liberals favour it
- why realists and liberals view the protection of human rights differently in international relations
- the way in which Hedley Bull's anarchical society theory provides a way of understanding why stability can exist within global politics
- how the works of Francis Fukuyama and Samuel Huntington contribute to the liberal/realist debate
- (although realism and liberalism are examined in section B) the need to approach contemporary developments in global politics within a realist/liberal context in both Section A and Section C.

2 The state and globalisation

The nation-state and national sovereignty

- A **nation-state** is an independent self-governing body whose citizens possess a shared identity based on factors such as language, ancestry and culture.
- A nation-state is also sovereign, which means that it has absolute authority over everything that occurs within its borders.
- According to realists, the sovereign nation-state is the most important actor in global politics. Although nation-states vary greatly in size and strength, they all possess the same sovereign right to govern themselves.
- How sovereign states react with each other, while protecting their **sovereignty**, has been likened to the way in which billiard balls collide with each other without damaging their outer shell.
- Realists say that since the nation-state claims sovereign power, there is therefore no authority greater than the nation-state.
- The 193 nation-states recognised by the United Nations (2019) represent the key actors in global politics.
- The primacy of the nation-state in global politics is in accord with Westphalian principles of state sovereignty. This is because the peace of Westphalia (1648), which ended the Thirty Years War, was based upon the recognition of the inviolability of state borders.

Nation-state is a sovereign political community defined by shared characteristics such as common heritage, identity, ethnicity and culture.

Sovereignty refers to absolute and unlimited legal authority. Nation-states have sovereign power within their national borders.

Exam tip

The centrality of the nation-state is a key element of realism and so students should be prepared to make strong references to realist political thought (covered in Chapter 1) when writing about national sovereignty.

The various types of globalisation

REVISED

Globalisation refers to the way in which the world becomes more closely connected. These connections are economic, political and cultural and have been dramatically advanced by the internet. Globalisation creates a complex web of interconnectivity which puts limits on the sovereign independence of nation-states.

Globalisation is the process through which the world becomes more closely interconnected and interdependent.

Economic globalisation

- **Economic globalisation** is the process through which the global economy becomes more closely connected by free trade.
- The principle of free trade is closely connected with neoclassical economic theory and is also known as the Washington Consensus.
- The Bretton Woods institutions (the World Bank, the International Monetary Fund and the World Trade Organization) drive forward economic globalisation by encouraging nation-states to reduce tariffs and embrace global trade.
- Economic globalisation has also been advanced by the growth of global financial markets. This has been facilitated by the internet so that capital can be instantaneously invested almost anywhere in the world. As a result, the prosperity of a nation-state is determined by the amount of foreign direct investment that it can attract.

Economic globalisation refers to the way in which the global economy becomes more closely connected and interdependent as a result of free trade and the increased cross-border transfer of goods, capital, services and workers.

Political globalisation

- **Political globalisation** refers to how nation-states increasingly share power. This suggests that the centrality of the nation-state in international relations is being complemented by new ways of reaching decisions.
- Intergovernmental organisations such as the United Nations, the World Trade Organization, the International Monetary Fund, the International Court of Justice (ICJ) and the G7 and G20 all provide opportunities for nation-states to collectively resolve shared dilemmas.
- Non-governmental organisations, such as Human Rights Watch, Save the Children and Friends of the Earth, also provide an important contribution to a global dialogue. Global media organisations, such as Fox Broadcasting, are highly influential in determining how international events are reported.
- International figures can advance political debate through the establishment of global agencies such as the Clinton Foundation. Global celebrities, such as Emma Watson, have contributed to a global debate about gender equality.
- Significant progress on developing innovatory approaches to reducing carbon emissions is being led by billionaires such as Bill Gates, Mark Zuckerberg and Jeff Bezos in the Breakthrough Energy Coalition.
- The way in which nation-states across the world have joined together in regional organisations further challenges the nation-state as the key actor in global politics. These organisations include advanced forms of regionalism such as the European Union, which is based on a common citizenship and has a common external tariff.
- Political globalisation creates a cobweb model of decision-making based on overlapping and mutually supporting bodies. It is polycentric because so many states and **non-state actors** are involved in the process.

Political globalisation refers to the way in which nation-states work with other nation-states and non-state actors through institutions of global governance, such as the United Nations, to reach collective decisions.

Non-state actors, such as non-governmental agencies, transnational corporations or lobbying groups which are not nation-states, are significant participants in global decision-making.

Cultural globalisation

- **Cultural globalisation** is the process by which the differences between cultures become less significant. This is the result of the popularisation of certain brands and trends across the world.
- This process is often referred to as Coca-Colonization. According to the sociologist Brendan Barber, cultural globalisation creates a 'McWorld' in which the rich variety of different global cultures is **homogenised** into a bland cultural experience.
- Cultural globalisation is also closely associated with materialism because globally people want access to the same consumer experience.
- It is also connected with Americanisation because of the way in which nation-states across the world have been so much influenced by the American cultural experience.

Cultural globalisation refers to the way in which nation-states display such cultural similarities that a collective global identity is created.

Homogenisation and monoculture suggest a blending of diverse cultures into a unified global culture based on shared experiences and a collective identity.

Now test yourself

TESTED

1. What are the key characteristics of a nation-state?
2. What is economic globalisation and how is it spread?
3. What is political globalisation and how is it spread?
4. Why is cultural globalisation associated with homogenisation and monoculture?

Answers on p. 106

Typical mistake

Students can fail to evaluate the impact of the various types of globalisation on the nation-state. Be prepared to explain which type of globalisation you think has had the biggest impact on state sovereignty.

In what ways does globalisation impact on the state system?

REVISED

The extent to which globalisation is changing the world is hotly disputed. The various arguments are outlined in Table 2.1.

- Some critics suggest that globalisation has dramatically reduced the centrality of the nation-state in global politics.
- Others argue that the nation-state remains the key actor in global politics and may even have been strengthened by globalisation.

Table 2.1 Hyperglobalisers, globalisation sceptics and transformationalists: the arguments on globalisation

Hyperglobalisers	• Hyperglobalisers argue that globalisation has led to a decisive readjustment in the location of power. • Growing trade connections, capital and information flows, cultural homogenisation and the rise of intergovernmental organisations have combined to undermine the importance of the nation-state. • The way in which the independent decision-making power of nation-states has been reduced by globalisation is leading to a post-sovereign state borderless world.
Globalisation sceptics	• Globalisation sceptics respond that the nation-state is still the key actor in global politics. • Nation-states are often reluctant to abandon their sovereignty to institutions of global governance such as the International Criminal Court. • The Trump administration's introduction of high tariffs to protect its industry from foreign competition demonstrates the limits of economic globalisation. • Governments in China (Xi), Russia (Putin), the United States (Trump) and Turkey (Erdogan) have achieved popularity by advancing nationalist policies and rejecting the shared cultural values associated with globalisation.
Transformationalists	• Transformationalists agree with hyperglobalisers that globalisation has irrevocably changed the world. However, they suggest that nation-states are adapting to globalisation rather than being 'hollowed out' by it. • This is shown by the way in which nation-states like the United States and China have become so powerful as a result of global free trade. • Instantaneous communication can also extend a nation-state's influence. Russia Today (RT) does this on behalf of Russia. Local cultures can adapt to, rather than be overwhelmed by, monoculture: Bollywood derives from Hollywood, but is culturally very distinct.

Exam tip

The terms hyperglobaliser, globalisation sceptic and transformationalist provide a helpful way of assessing the relative impact of globalisation and should therefore be used at key points in your writing.

How liberals and realists view globalisation

REVISED

The different views of liberals and realists on globalisation are outlined in Table 2.2.

Table 2.2 How do liberals and realists view globalisation?

Liberals	Realists
Liberals are positive about globalisation because they believe that it encourages global cooperation, peace and understanding. As a result of trading and investing freely with each other the differences between nation-states are 'flattened out' and conflict becomes less likely. 'If goods do not cross borders, armies will' – Frédéric Bastiat, 1801–1850). By working with each other in intergovernmental organs such as the United Nations, the World Trade Organization and regional organisations, nation-states learn to value the collective good over national self-interest. This is important in challenging state egoism. Cultural globalisation also spreads liberal values based on individual self-fulfilment. This challenges autocratic and semi-autocratic governments and leads to the rise of democracies. This further encourages peace and stability because democracies are unlikely to go to war with each other.	Realists are sceptical about globalisation. They believe in the primacy of the nation-state and oppose any reduction in its sovereign power and influence. Realists therefore believe that nation-states should engage in free trade if it is to their advantage. If it is not, then there is a strong case for tariffs and subsidies because the nation-state's loyalty is to its citizens, not to the global community. Since the nation-state is sovereign it should not allow its sovereignty to be compromised by undemocratic regional organisations and intergovernmental organisations. Instead, nation-states should always approach global problems according to the national interest. Realists value the unique cultural inheritance of each nation-state. They oppose the rise of a global monoculture because it challenges the right of the nation-state to be the main influence on the cultural experience of its citizens.

How is the sovereign influence of the nation-state challenged by globalisation?

REVISED

The impact of economic globalisation

- Since the end of the Cold War (1991) countries across the world have embraced the principles of neoclassical economic liberalism.
- This has limited the economic choices available to nation-states since in order to attract trade and investment, they need to conform to the main free-market principles of the Washington Consensus.
- For example, nation-states have a strong incentive to keep corporation taxation low and to lightly regulate business since this will encourage foreign investment.
- World Bank and International Monetary Fund structural adjustment programmes require recipient nation-states to adopt free-market reforms. These include privatisation, cutting taxes and reducing the role of the state in the economy.
- The decisions that international investors make over where to invest, and where transnational corporations will open and close factories, are crucial in determining the prosperity of a nation-state.
- The effect on nation-states across the world of the financial crash caused by the collapse of Lehman Brothers (2008) demonstrates how tightly economic globalisation has linked the world economy.
- The economic fortunes of nation-states are therefore often determined by forces beyond the control of their governments.

The limits of economic globalisation

- Although nation-states cannot avoid globalisation, they can still try to manipulate it to their advantage or limit its influence.

- China has ignored global criticisms that it has devalued its currency so that it can boost its exports.
- The Trump administration pulled out of the Trans-Pacific Partnership because it did not believe that it served the USA's economic interests.
- In order to protect American industry, in 2018 the Trump administration also placed a 25% tariff on steel imports and a 10% tariff on aluminium imports. China, the European Union and Canada quickly responded with their own retaliatory tariffs.
- This demonstrates the way in which nation-states can abandon the principles of free trade if it conflicts with what they see as being to their economic advantage.
- Economic globalisation has threatened job security in the European Union and this has led to the growing popularity of populist movements which are designed to protect workers' rights and security.
- In 2018, President Macron of France, for example, was forced to make concessions to the *gilets jaunes* (the yellow jackets) as a result of their anti-globalisation protests. The concessions included an increase in the minimum wage, to be paid for by a national tax on transnational corporations such as Apple, Google, Facebook and Amazon.

The impact of political globalisation

- By establishing intergovernmental organisations and involving non-state actors and non-governmental organisations in collective decision-making, political globalisation challenges the centrality of the nation-state in global politics.

Intergovernmental organisations

- Intergovernmental organisations such as the United Nations, the International Court of Justice and the World Trade Organization provide opportunities for a collective response to shared problems.
- According to United Nations Responsibility to Protect (2005), the sovereignty of nation-states is conditional upon them not committing mass human rights abuses. If they do, then the international community is justified in intervening to stop them.
- The growth of regional organisations, such as the European Union and the Association of Southeast Asian Nations (ASEAN), shows how nation-states are prepared to pool their sovereignty in order to advance their collective interests.

Non-governmental organisations

- Non-state actors are now advancing the political debate. In 2018, Jeff Bezos, the founder of Amazon, was named the fifth most influential person in the world. Bezos has set up his own space exploration venture, Blue Origin, to utilise the resources of space 'in order to preserve Earth'.
- Climate change activist Greta Thunberg addressed The United Nations in 2019. Her campaign has provoked mass global support in favour of more action to combat climate change. This shows how individuals are taking the initiative on issues which nation-states have previously led on.
- Non-governmental organisations, such as Greenpeace and Human Rights Watch, play a vital role in advancing a global dialogue on pressing issues.

- The Gates, Clinton and Carter Foundations work with nation-states to resolve collective dilemmas. The Carter Foundation, for example, has been responsible for the almost global eradication of the guinea worm disease.

The limits of political globalisation

- However, nation-states still exert considerable influence over their domestic affairs and often put their own interests before those of the global community.
- Nation-states can ignore the decisions of the International Court of Justice and the European Court of Human Rights. The International Criminal Court has been condemned by President Trump as having 'an unelected, unaccountable global bureaucracy'.
- International treaties such as the Nuclear Non-Proliferation Treaty (1968) and the Paris Climate Change Agreement (2015) require the cooperation of nation-states to be effective. In 2017, the Trump administration withdrew the United States from the Paris Accord. Pakistan and India have both broken the Nuclear Non-Proliferation Treaty by developing a nuclear capability.
- Although UN Responsibility to Protect (2005) states that sovereignty is conditional on the protection of human rights, humanitarian interventions *within* sovereign states are rare. Nation-states therefore *practically* retain complete control over human rights provision within their borders.
- European federalism is being challenged by the rise of nationalist movements in member states such as Hungary, Italy and Poland, highlighting the enduring importance of the nation-state.
- The possession of national sovereignty, in spite of globalisation, still matters in international relations. We can see this in regard to competing claims over Gibraltar by Spain and the UK and the way in which Russia annexed Crimea from Ukraine in 2014. As China becomes more powerful it is increasingly pressing its claims on the ownership of Taiwan.

The impact of cultural globalisation

- The spread of global brands such as Disney, Apple and Microsoft has helped to establish a global monoculture based upon shared cultural experiences. This challenges the nation-state's dominance of its citizens' cultural experience.
- The popularity of global celebrities and the universal appeal of Hollywood films are further creating a homogenised world culture.
- Instagram and Twitter enable celebrities to have a global following. YouTube makes it possible for a global audience to have the same viewing experience. This is challenging the influence of national broadcasting companies such as the BBC.
- All of this undermines cultural diversity and replaces it with a uniform global culture based on brand-centred consumerism and materialism.

The limits of cultural globalisation

- Nevertheless, nation-states can still command the cultural allegiance of their citizens and nationalism continues to provide a powerful way of achieving a sense of group identity and belonging.
- The success of Bollywood demonstrates how nation-states like India can adapt global culture to their own national traditions.

- Cultural globalisation has even created a backlash in favour of the traditional values of nation-states.
- Viktor Orbán's emphasis on the importance of Hungary's Christian heritage has contributed to his hold on power. In Italy, Poland, Sweden, Germany and France, nationalist parties have achieved success by rejecting global monoculture.
- In Russia, President Putin has contrasted the values of the Orthodox Church with 'decadent' Western liberalism.
- Although certain brands have a global appeal, this only creates a superficial global culture. For example, the way in which homosexual acts are a criminal offence in 73 nation-states (2019) shows how nation-states still determine their national cultural values.

Exam tip

Nationalism is one of the non-core ideologies examined in Unit Two. Even if you are not studying it as your chosen ideology you could study some of its core thinkers in order to understand the way in which nationalism can generate such powerful loyalty to the nation-state.

Debate

Does economic globalisation resolve global poverty?

Yes	No
Economic liberalism/free trade encourages more trade and this encourages greater global wealth. Global competition drives down prices, so benefiting consumers. All nation-states have a comparative advantage in goods, expertise or their labour force which they can utilise in the global marketplace. The developing world has taken advantage of new trading and manufacturing opportunities to achieve greater convergence with the developed world. The economic growth of China, India, South Korea and Turkey has been as a result of the economic opportunities of globalisation. India was the world's fastest growing economy in 2018–2019 (7.3%). Its young, English-proficient workforce is making it dominant in the global service industry. Vietnam's low labour costs are attracting investment from transnational corporations such as Samsung. The Vietnamese economy grew by 7% in 2018. East Africa is also benefiting from low labour costs as transnational corporations open factories there. This has meant that the economy diversifies away from subsistence agriculture towards manufacturing. In 2018, Nissan announced that it was going to start building cars in Kenya.	According to dependency theory, economic globalisation represents neocolonialism. This is because advanced economies (the Global North) exploit the workforces and raw materials of the developing world (the Global South). As a result, the developing world becomes dependent on cheap mass-produced products from the developed world. Therefore, those countries do not achieve industrialisation themselves. Small farmers and artisans have their livelihoods ruined by global conglomerates. Economic globalisation creates a 'race to the bottom' because nation-states reduce workers' protection in order to attract investment. The collapse of the Rana Plaza factory (2013) in Bangladesh was caused by inadequate building safeguards due to cost-cutting. Leading companies such as Walmart and Foxconn subcontract production to factories where workers' rights can be poorly protected. The Foxconn factory in Longhua, which makes Apple products, employs 450,000 people. It has been criticised for harsh working conditions. In 2010 there was a spate of suicides at the factory. Workers' rates of pay are kept to a minimum as transnational corporations locate to where labour costs are lowest.

→

Yes	No
In 2017, exports from developing countries increased by 12%, reaching 43% of world trade. The value of world trade in 2005 was $8 trillion. In 2013 it was $18.8 trillion. More people have been lifted out of poverty by globalisation than by anything else. The relative success of the Millennium Goals is primarily due to economic globalisation.	The more successful neocolonial power in the world is China. It is the biggest investor in Africa and South America, but its mines and factories have a poor record on protecting workers' rights. Although economic globalisation creates greater wealth, it mostly goes to shareholders in transnational corporations, resulting in greater global inequality. Economic globalisation does not raise all boats equally.

Exam tip

The debate on economic globalisation is further covered in global economic governance (Chapter 4).

Now test yourself

TESTED

5 Why is economic globalisation (the Washington Consensus) so controversial?
6 Give examples of nation-states making collective decisions through intergovernmental organisations.
7 Why and in what ways has there been a negative reaction against cultural globalisation?
8 Give examples of the nation-state still determining what occurs within its borders.

Answers on pp. 106–7

Typical mistake

Students need to appreciate that economic globalisation is a highly controversial issue. Therefore they need to avoid writing one-sided essays. Instead they should impartially evaluate the advantages *and* disadvantages of economic globalisation.

Crimes against humanity refers to a systematic and planned attempt to inflict large-scale suffering on a civilian population through policies such as widespread murder, genocide, enslavement, imprisonment, torture or expulsion from their homes.

Exam tip

The relationship between the nation-state and globalisation should be placed within a liberal/realist context whenever possible.

Debate

Have there been significant advances in the global protection of human rights?

Yes	No
As the world becomes more interconnected because of globalisation, there has been a greater focus on universal standards of human rights.	It is rare for nation-states to accept outside intervention in cases involving human rights. Westphalian principles of national sovereignty ensure that nation-states determine the extent of human rights within their borders.

➜

Yes	No
In 1993, the Office of the United Nations High Commissioner for Human Rights was established to encourage global respect for human rights. In 2005, the United Nations General Assembly endorsed UN Responsibility to Protect. This states that if sovereign nation-states commit systematic human rights abuses then the international community has the responsibility to intervene. A number of humanitarian interventions have taken place to protect human rights. These include Kosovo (1999), East Timor (1999–2000), Sierra Leone (2000), Libya (2011) and Mali (2013–2014). UN tribunals (the former Yugoslavia, Sierra Leone, Rwanda, Cambodia) have developed international standards of human rights law. The International Criminal Court (2002) is a permanent body and can initiate prosecutions of war crimes if nation-states do not do this. Advances in technology ensure that human rights abuses are better documented than ever before. In 2017 and 2018, the United States launched missile attacks on the Syrian government following its alleged use of chemical weapons. Pressure groups such as Human Rights Watch globally monitor human rights abuses. The internet also enables movements such as the 'He For She' campaign to achieve global influence. Transnational corporations such as Nike and Levi Strauss have improved their record on corporate social responsibility as a result of the negative publicity that their factories were receiving on the internet.	This means that the United Nations Declaration of Human Rights is 'soft' not 'hard' law. In the same way, the European Convention on Human Rights has no binding power on member states of the Council of Europe. Although the International Criminal Court has successfully prosecuted some **crimes against humanity**, influential nation-states such as the United States, Russia and China do not recognise its legitimacy. It is especially difficult to hold powerful nation-states accountable for any human rights abuses which they may have committed. Alleged human rights abuses committed during the Syrian civil war by Syrian government and Russian forces have not been prosecuted. In the same way Saudi Arabia has not been held accountable for human rights abuses which it has been accused of committing during its intervention in Yemen. Critics claim that the United Nations Human Rights Council is unable to fulfil its functions because its members include nation-states with a poor record on human rights, such as Saudi Arabia. As a result of different cultural traditions, the extent to which women's rights and the rights of LGBT people are protected vary greatly across the world. Although Human Rights Watch exposes human rights abuses, it has no enforcement power. The growing self-confidence of Russia and China on the UN Security Council will make it more difficult to enforce human rights. They oppose liberal humanitarian interventions and prioritise the importance of state sovereignty.

Globalisation and conflict

REVISED

- Liberals claim that globalisation reduces conflict. This is because political globalisation enables nation-states to cooperate in intergovernmental organisations, including the ICJ and the WTO, to resolve collective dilemmas.
- Economic globalisation creates so many supply-chain connections between nation-states that it would be irrational for them to go to war with each other. The economist Thomas Friedman has called this the Dell Theory of Conflict Prevention.
- However, although economic globalisation increases global wealth, it distributes that wealth very unequally. This creates resentments within and between nation-states.
- As the developing world becomes economically more powerful as a result of globalisation, this leads to unemployment in traditional manufacturing industries in the developed world.

- The loss of these jobs to the developing world has been a key factor in the rise of nationalist parties in Europe and President Trump's 'America first' commitment.
- This creates an economic conflict of interests between the developed and the developing worlds. This is evidenced by the trade war between China and the United States, which broke out as a result of President Trump's imposition of extensive tariffs on Chinese exports to the United States.
- Global and regional migration has led to new competition for jobs. This has also led to the rise of nationalist parties such as the French National Front and Alternative for Germany.
- The internet facilitates the spread of extremist ideas such as Islamism and right-wing nationalism which threaten conflict. It also enables nation-states to threaten each other with cyber technology, so creating a new technological arms race.

Globalisation and the environment

REVISED

- Globalisation has led to world industrialisation. This has contributed to a dramatic increase in global carbon emissions as coal is the main source of fuel in the industrialisation of the developing world.
- Global interconnectivity has led to a huge increase in air travel. Plane fuel is thought to be one of the world's worst polluters.
- Transnational corporations can have a negative impact on the environment. Shell has been criticised for the environmental degradation of the Niger Delta. Environmental groups are highly critical of the impact of fracking.
- Globalisation encourages consumerism and materialism and so contributes to increasing global waste.
- Globalisation has lifted people out of poverty and increased life expectancy and this has led to a significant increase in the global population. This puts more strains on the environment as humans consume more and increase waste.
- More intense agricultural cultivation to feed the growing population leads to desertification. Europe is increasingly facing large migrant flows from North Africa as land becomes exhausted.
- However, political globalisation provides a way of responding to this problem. Global climate change conferences have established that climate change is a 'collective dilemma'.
- In 2015, the Paris Climate Change Agreement established a global commitment by nation-states to keep temperature increase in the twenty-first century below two degrees and as close to 1.5 degrees as possible.
- Globalisation encourages the spread of ideas and innovation. In 2015 Bill Gates set up Breakthrough Energy Ventures to develop carbon-neutral energy development.
- Economic globalisation drives down the price of energy-saving products because they can be manufactured in low-cost countries. In 2018, China built half the world's electric cars.
- The internet has provided climate change activists like Greta Thunberg and Extinction Rebellion with the opportunity to inspire a global mass movement in favour of faster action on climage change.

Exam tip

Be aware of the significance of debates between leading political theorists. In *The Rise of the Civilizational State* (2019) Christopher Coker argues that China is becoming more nationalistically assertive as a result of the wealth it has gained through successfully engaging in economic globalisation. This contrasts with Francis Fukuyama's much more optimistic interpretation of globalisation in *The End of History* (1992), which is covered in Chapter 1.

Debate

Is globalisation a way of advancing Western interests?

Yes	No
Since the end of the Cold War (1991) globalisation has generally been seen as a way of advancing Western economic, political and cultural interests. The Bretton Woods institutions (World Bank, International Monetary Fund and World Trade Organization) have spread the free-market principles of the Washington Consensus. This is to the advantage of Western transnational corporations because they have been able to trade anywhere in the world. The top ten most admired companies in the world are all American (2019). The spread of free markets has encouraged the spread of liberal democracy. When the Cold War ended, Francis Fukuyama predicted that free trade would lead to global liberalisation as autocratic governments were replaced by democracies. This occurred in eastern Europe and South America. Cultural globalisation is closely connected with Americanisation. This is the process whereby American cultural values and brands achieve a world following. McDonald's, Nike, Disney, Facebook and Starbucks are all examples of global success.	The fastest-growing economies are in the Global South. This is leading to greater convergence between the developing and the developed worlds. Manufacturing jobs in the Global North are increasingly being lost to the Global South. This is why the Trump administration has introduced tariffs to protect the country from competition, especially from China. China is becoming a global economic and military superpower as a result of globalisation. China's one-party government and lack of democracy directly challenge Western liberal and democratic values. Three of the top five most wealthy companies in the world are Chinese (2018). The Beijing Consensus of state-run capitalism based on an absence of political freedom is increasingly challenging the more liberal Washington Consensus. The internet enables other cultural ideologies to challenge the United States' influence. RT advances a highly nationalist world view. Islamism has utilised social media to gain a global following. American-led liberalism and consumerism have provoked a backlash in favour of more conservative world views such as Islam. The Arab Risings generally led to a rise in religious conservatism rather than liberal democracy.

Debate

Has globalisation widened and deepened global interconnectedness/interdependence?

Yes	No
Hyperglobalisers argue that globalisation is creating a 'post-sovereign state' world. Economic and cultural globalisation is establishing a 'borderless world'. This is because nation-states can no longer insulate themselves from outside influences. State borders are now more porous.	In spite of globalisation there are still significant barriers and differences between nation-states. Rather than creating a 'global village', economic globalisation creates resentment and encourages nationalism. Nationalist parties in Europe have won support by promising to protect society from migrant labour.

→

Yes	No
Global free trade has created an interconnected world economy. As a result of advances in technology, capital also passes instantaneously between nation-states. This means that the economic and financial health of nation-states is interdependent. The Bretton Woods institutions (World Bank, International Monetary Fund and World Trade Organization) have helped to make the principles of the Washington Consensus universal. A homogenised global culture based on materialism, consumerism, celebrity and brand recognition has been created. This has diluted the differences between cultures, establishing a McWorld of cultural uniformity. As a result of cultural globalisation, certain brands, such as Nike, Coca-Cola and Google, possess a world following. Facebook had 2.32 billion monthly active users in 2018. 2.2 billion iPhones had been sold by 2018, making it the world's most popular product. The nation-state is now having to share power with non-state actors in institutions of global governance such as the United Nations and the World Trade Organization. Global problems require collective solutions. In 2005, UN Responsibility to Protect established the principle that the international community can intervene within nation-states to ensure the protection of human rights. The Paris Climate Change Agreement (2015) created a global consensus that nation-states must work together to resolve the threat from climate change.	President Trump's commitment to building a wall between Mexico and the United States demonstrates the limits of globalisation. Economic globalisation has also made manufacturing jobs in the developed world less secure, leading to the protectionism of the Trump administration. Regional organisations, such as the European Union and ASEAN, represent the economic interests of the nation-states in them. They are not supposed to foster global interdependence. The European Union's high external tariff has led to it being referred to as 'fortress Europe'. Intergovernmental organs lack supranational authority. Nation-states usually approach them according to their national self-interest. They thus fail to make the world more interdependent. For example, the International Court of Justice and the International Criminal Court both lack coercive power. The principles of UN Responsibility to Protect (2005) have been ignored in the Syrian civil war. Nation-states can use the internet to advance their national interests. RT provides a partisan Russo-centric interpretation of global events. Russia and China have also been accused of using cyber technology to undermine liberal democracies. The Chinese company Huawei has been accused of using its electronic technology to undermine the security of the countries that use its products. This demonstrates how globalisation can increase tension and foster distrust between nation-states. Globalisation has made China more economically and politically powerful. This has made it more assertively nationalist over Taiwan and the Senkaku/Diaoyu islands.

Now test yourself

TESTED

9 What is the significance of UN Responsibility to Protect (2005)? How much of an impact has it had on international relations?
10 In what ways are human rights protected in international relations? How effective are these safeguards?
11 In what ways has globalisation had a positive/negative impact on the environment?
12 Why has globalisation been accused of increasing global tensions?

Answers on p. 107

Exam tip

Supranationalism refers to an institution which can compel the obedience of a nation-state. It is covered more completely in Chapter 8 on regionalism and the European Union.

Exam practice

Section A

1 Examine the ways in which the sovereignty of the nation-state has been challenged by economic and political globalisation. [12]

2 Examine the differences between economic and political globalisation. [12]

Section C

3 Evaluate the extent to which the nation-state no longer plays the central role in global politics. [30]

4 Evaluate the extent to which globalisation has positively reshaped global relations. [30]

5 Evaluate the extent to which economic globalisation is effective in combatting global poverty. [30]

6 Evaluate the extent to which cultural globalisation has had a bigger impact on the world than economic globalisation. [30]

Answers and quick quiz 2 online

ONLINE

Summary

You should now have an understanding of the following:

- what sovereignty means and why it is so important in international relations
- the distinction between economic, political and cultural globalisation
- why liberals and realists view globalisation differently
- the ways in which hyperglobalisers, globalisation sceptics and transformationalists approach globalisation differently
- whether globalisation has challenged the centrality of the nation-state in international relations
- the extent to which globalisation has been successful in reducing global poverty
- whether global conflict has been reduced as a result of political globalisation
- whether the impact of cultural globalisation has been more positive or negative.

3 Global governance: political

The United Nations

The enormous conflict and suffering which the Second World War (1939–1945) provoked encouraged the establishment of the **United Nations** as a way of developing a more liberal approach to resolving global crises.

The Charter of the United Nations (1945) lays down the main priorities of the United Nations:

- the maintenance of global peace and security
- the encouragement of closer relations between nation-states
- greater respect for human rights and international law
- the global encouragement of social and economic wellbeing.

The United Nations is a liberal organ of global governance. It was established in 1945 to maintain global peace and security, promote human rights, and encourage economic and social development.

The United Nations Security Council

REVISED

- Although the head of the United Nations is the Secretary-General (António Guterres, 2017–), it is the **Security Council** that wields the most influence in issues to do with conflict.
- There are 15 members of the Security Council. The most important are the five permanent members, each of which possesses the right of veto. These are the United States, Russia, China, the United Kingdom and France.
- In addition to the permanent five there are ten non-veto-wielding members. These are elected by the General Assembly of the United Nations for a two-year term.
- The Security Council is so important because the Charter of the United Nations provides it with the key executive role in maintaining global peace and security.
- Under Chapter 7 of the UN Charter, the Security Council determines what action should be taken in response to 'threats to the peace, breaches of the peace or acts of aggression'.
- In these circumstances legally binding Security Council resolutions can authorise the establishment of peacekeeping missions and impose sanctions on nation-states. In 2019, there were 16 UN peacekeeping missions operational. These included Kosovo, Afghanistan, Darfur, the Democratic Republic of the Congo and Mali.
- In rare circumstances, the Security Council can sanction military force against a member state which has committed an act of aggression against another member state.
- In 1950, Chapter 7 was used to justify military action against North Korea for invading South Korea. In 1991, it was also used to legitimise the first Gulf War when Iraqi forces were expelled from Kuwait by a US-led UN force.
- However, critics of the Security Council argue that the permanent five are too often ready to prioritise realist self-interest, so undermining the liberal good intentions of the UN Charter.

The Security Council is responsible for the maintenance of global peace and security. It has five permanent veto-wielding members and ten rotating members who determine how the United Nations should respond to threats to peace.

Debate

Is the Security Council effective in preventing and resolving conflict?

No	Yes
The main problem with the Security Council is that the decisions of the permanent five can be determined by realist self-interest. During the genocide in Rwanda (1994), the Security Council was unwilling to intervene. The United States, in particular, was unprepared to commit to a military response since the deaths of 18 US servicemen on a humanitarian mission in Somalia in 1993. Since the outbreak of the Syrian civil war in 2011, as a close ally of President Assad, Russia has used its veto to oppose military intervention within Syria. Even when the Security Council *does* agree on military intervention it does not have its own military force and so has to request forces from the member states. This can take a considerable amount of time as a crisis is unfolding. Once military action is taken it often fails to achieve much success, especially when intervention is in a war zone. This is because UN forces can be under-resourced or do not have a sufficiently robust mandate to intervene to stop the killing. The way in which the geostrategic interests of China and Russia are increasingly in conflict with those of the United States, the United Kingdom and France is likely to make it more difficult for the Security Council to agree on conflict resolution in the future. In 2013, the Security Council did demand that the Syrian government abandon its chemical weapon programme. However, the Security Council could not agree on whether this had occurred. When the Trump administration, in 2017 and 2018, bombed alleged Syrian chemical weapons sites, it was condemned by Russia for violating Syrian sovereignty.	UN peacekeeping operations can be successful if the Security Council agrees to wholeheartedly support them. They need to be well-resourced, with an effective mandate and achievable objectives. The support of the local population is also very important to the success of a peacekeeping mission. UN resolution 678 in 1990 mandated military action to expel Iraqi forces from Kuwait. Following the liberation of Kuwait in 1991, UN Resolution 688 was used to establish safe havens in Iraq to stop Saddam Hussein launching attacks upon the Iraqi Kurds. UN Resolution 1973 in 2011 mandated the establishment of a no-fly zone in Libya to protect the civilian population. NATO then, controversially, used this as a justification for military action against the government of Colonel Gaddafi. From 2006 to 2015 the Security Council imposed extensive economic sanctions on Iran which forced it to negotiate with the international community on the abandonment of its nuclear weapons programme. In 2015, Security Council Resolution 2253 agreed extensive financial measures to stop the funding of terrorist organisations such as al-Qaeda and so-called Islamic State. The Security Council is most effective in resolving conflict when the interests of its members coincide. In these circumstances the permanent five will not need to exercise their right of veto.

The most visible way in which the United Nations attempts to encourage peace and stability is through its peacekeeping operations. The extent to which they are successful is hotly disputed, however (see Table 3.1).

Table 3.1 The UN as peacekeeper: the successes and failures

UN peacekeeping failures	UN peacekeeping successes
In Bosnia in the 1990s UN forces lacked an effective mandate to take offensive military action. This is why the 'safe haven' of Srebrenica fell to Bosnian Serb forces in 1995. UN forces in Darfur have also not been allowed to take military action against Sudanese government forces even when they have been accused of widespread atrocities. In 2019 UN peacekeeping missions in Kashmir and Afghanistan had only a tiny number of military personnel. UN peacekeepers in Afghanistan reported that 3804 civilians were killed in 2018: the highest number so far. Although 19,000 UN peacekeepers (military and non-military) are operating in the Democratic Republic of the Congo (2019), the size of the country and unresolved tribal and ethnic hostilities have undermined their effectiveness.	The Australian-led UN intervention in East Timor (1999–2000) was effective in supporting the country's transition to democracy. Peacekeeping troops effectively disarmed criminal gangs and rebel groups. A large-scale UN intervention in Côte d'Ivoire (12,000 personnel in 2011), spearheaded by France, was successful in disarming rival military groups and re-establishing democracy following civil war. From 2003 to 2018, UN peacekeepers in Liberia were successful in implementing the peace process. The support of the population and the robust mandate of the peacekeepers enabled the success. The relatively small size of all these countries and the significant size of the peacekeeping operations all contributed to the overall success of these missions.

- As a result of its mixed record on conflict resolution there have been a number of calls for the Security Council to be reformed. The main criticism of the Security Council is that it gives too much power to the permanent five.
- For a decision to be reached there needs to be a two-thirds majority of the permanent and non-permanent members. However, each member of the permanent five can exercise the veto, making it much more difficult to achieve consensus.
- The fact that the five **great powers** on the Security Council all possess the veto means that they can never have UN military action taken against them if they threaten the peace. For example, the annexation of Crimea by Russia in 2014 was condemned by 13 members of the Security Council in 2014. It did not pass because Russia vetoed it and China abstained.
- The privileged status of the permanent five challenges the principle of the 'sovereign equality of all its members' (UN Charter).
- Consequently, there is a strong case that the Security Council needs to be reformed in order for it to be able to intervene more often and effectively to deter or stop conflict. It also needs to recognise that the permanent five ought to be held responsible for their actions in the same way as less powerful nation-states.

A great power has strong regional and global influence. It will play a major role in intergovernmental organisations and will be fully engaged in the resolution of international problems, crises and conflicts.

Debate

Should the Security Council be reformed?

Yes	No
The fact that each permanent member of the Security Council possesses the right of veto means that it is very difficult to achieve a consensus on military action.	Having just five permanent veto-wielding members of the Security Council means it is important that a consensus is reached before economic sanctions are imposed or military action is taken.

→

Yes	No
This is especially the case in conflicts in which members of the permanent five have a geostrategic interest.	As a result, the case for intervention has to be very strong. In 2003, the Security Council did not accept that there was sufficient justification for war against Iraq.
For example, Russia supports the government of Syria and China has close relations with Myanmar. Therefore, neither is likely to support UN intervention in these humanitarian crises.	If decisions were to be made by a simple or qualified majority, then the case for action would not need to be so conclusive.
The membership of the Security Council represents the balance of power in 1945. It does not take into account how the balance of power has changed since then and so its decisions lack legitimacy.	Although UN interventions therefore might be more numerous, they might not be as well-justified. This would encourage the likelihood of the great powers removing their support from the United Nations since they would have less control over it.
The claims of France and the UK to be on the Security Council are controversial given their reduced global influence.	If the permanent membership of the Security Council was increased it would be difficult to decide which nation-states should be represented. On what criteria would the decision be reached?
There is a strong case for the developing world to be better represented on the Security Council.	
If it had broader representation, then the decisions of the Security Council might be less influenced by the geostrategic interests of powerful nation-states.	Changing the permanent membership would encourage considerable resentment. Pakistan, for example, strongly opposes India becoming a permanent member of the Security Council.
The principle of the great power veto means that none of the permanent five can be held accountable for instigating conflict because they would, of course, veto the resolution against them.	If the veto power were to be extended to other nation-states it would make it even more difficult to achieve consensus.

Exam tip

Revise the effectiveness of the UN Security Council in resolving conflict with human rights and humanitarian intervention (Chapter 5). These topics reinforce each other.

The United Nations General Assembly

REVISED

- Unlike the Security Council, all member states of the United Nations are equally represented on the General Assembly. This means that each nation-state, whatever its power, possesses the same influence.
- The General Assembly decides on the allocation of the UN budget and appoints the Secretary-General. Member states address the UN General Assembly and this can stimulate an international dialogue about pressing issues. The General Assembly can pass non-binding resolutions on any issue within the scope of the United Nations.
- The General Assembly's main function therefore is to represent world opinion. Its strengths and weaknesses are presented in Table 3.2.

Table 3.2 The strengths and weaknesses of the United Nations General Assembly

Strengths	Weaknesses
The General Assembly is the only place where all nations of the world can come together and engage in a genuinely global dialogue. The General Assembly enables the global community to highlight and seek consensus on important global issues. Its resolutions carry significant global weight and authority as they represent world opinion. In 2000, the General Assembly endorsed the Millennium Development Goals. In 2015, the General Assembly agreed to replace these with new Sustainable Development Goals until 2030. In 2005 at its World Summit, the General Assembly unanimously agreed to UN Responsibility to Protect. This states that 'each individual state has the responsibility to protect its populations from genocide, war crimes, ethnic cleansing and crimes against humanity'. During the 73rd session of the General Assembly in 2018, 146 nation-states emphasised the importance of combatting climate change. The equal voting rights that all member states have on the General Assembly means that the rights of smaller states are better recognised. In 2018, the presidents of small island states in the Caribbean, Pacific and Indian oceans urged the General Assembly to fulfil the terms of the Paris Treaty as they were being the first to suffer from climate change.	The resolutions of the General Assembly are non-binding. This means that the General Assembly lacks coercive power. The voting equality of member states on the General Assembly can also be seen as a weakness. Critics argue that it is irrational that a tiny city state such as Monaco carries as much influence on the General Assembly as the United States. On important issues such as conflict resolution the General Assembly plays a much more marginal role than the Security Council. Nation-states can advance realist self-interest on the General Assembly instead of seeking global consensus. World leaders can use the General Assembly to verbally abuse their enemies and try to win global support for themselves. For example, in 2018, President Trump used his speech to the General Assembly to attack Iran's leadership for spreading 'chaos, death and destruction'. In his speech to the General Assembly, President Rouhani then attacked Trump's 'weakness of intellect'. In his speech to the General Assembly in 2018, Prime Minister Netanyahu of Israel sought to protect Israel's national interests by taking the opportunity to 'expose' Iran's 'secret atomic warehouse'.

Now test yourself

TESTED

1. How effective is the UN Security Council in preventing conflict?
2. What are the main differences between the functions and powers of the UN Security Council and the UN General Assembly?
3. How convincing is the case for the reform of the UN Security Council?
4. Provide examples of the liberal intentions of the United Nations being undermined by nation-states pursuing a realist foreign policy.

Answers on p. 107

The International Court of Justice

REVISED

- The International Court of Justice was established in 1945 and is the judicial arm of the United Nations.
- It arbitrates disputes between member states and non-state actors and can request that the ICJ provides advisory opinions on contentious issues.

- The ICJ can be seen as a liberal organ of global governance trying to establish global respect for the rule of law.
- In order to be successful it is necessary that nation-states accept the judgments of the ICJ. In 2013, Thailand accepted an ICJ judgment that the disputed Preah Vihear temple belonged to Cambodia and that Thai troops would have to be withdrawn from it.
- However, nation-states generally put national self-interest first and so will often be unwilling to accept the judgment of the ICJ if it is against their interests.
- In 2019, the ICJ ruled that the British control of the Chagos Islands in the Indian Ocean is illegal. However, the UK government responded that the decision was only advisory and that possession of the Chagos Islands was vital to Britain's defence.

Exam tip

The International Court of Justice is covered in greater detail in Chapter 5: Global governance: human rights.

The Economic and Social Council

REVISED

- The Economic and Social Council (ECOSOC) coordinates the United Nations' commitment to economic, social and environmental development. Its strengths and weaknesses are outlined in Table 3.3.
- The General Assembly elects the 54 nation-states which make up the ECOSOC. Member states sit for three-year terms and seats on the ECOSOC are allocated to favour representation from the developing world.
- ECOSOC is designed to provide the developing world with greater influence over how development is carried out.
- The work of UN agencies such as the World Health Organization (WHO), the Office of the UN High Commissioner for Refugees (UNHCR) and the World Food Programme (WFP) is monitored by the Economic and Social Council.

Table 3.3 The strengths and weaknesses of the Economic and Social Council

Strengths	Weaknesses
The UN agencies which ECOSOC monitors play an important role in encouraging global development. The World Health Organization has coordinated global efforts to eradicate polio and combat leprosy. The World Food Programme is the biggest global humanitarian operation, delivering more than 15 billion emergency food rations each year. In 2017, there were 68.5 million displaced people in the world. The UNHCR plays the leading role in providing them with support and protection. It is the main body coordinating assistance to refugees in conflict zones such as the Middle East and South Sudan. ECOSOC has also set up new agencies such as UNAIDS to respond to the HIV/AIDS challenge. Sessions of ECOSOC each highlight an important developmental theme. In 2019, the theme was 'empowering people to build equal and inclusive societies'.	ECOSOC lacks a policy-making function. Critics claim it is primarily a global bureaucracy to which many different agencies report without a sense of overall coherence or vision. Its president sits for only one year, which means that it lacks the capacity for forward planning. Although the developing world is given most influence on ECOSOC, the principal decision-makers on how development should take place are the World Bank, the International Monetary Fund and the World Trade Organization. Developing countries are much less influential on these bodies. Rhonda King, ECOSOC president (2018–2019), stated it needs to have more of a 'deliberative function'. The large number of agencies which report to ECOSOC and often operate in the same country means that there can be a costly overlapping of responsibility and accountability.

In what ways does the United Nations protect human rights?

REVISED

- The United Nations Universal Declaration of Human Rights is the world's most powerful and comprehensive statement of human rights. In 1966 the United Nations adopted the International Covenant on Civil and Political Rights and the International Covenant on Economic, Social and Cultural Rights. Together these three documents comprise the International Bill of Human Rights.
- United Nations tribunals have been established to try human rights abuses committed in former Yugoslavia, Rwanda, Sierra Leone and Cambodia.
- The Relationship Agreement between the United Nations and the International Criminal Court (2002) states that they 'shall cooperate closely whenever appropriate'.
- In 2005, the UN World Summit endorsed UN Responsibility to Protect which provides the international community with the authority to intervene in nation-states where systematic human rights abuses are being carried out.
- The UNHCR and the Human Rights Council work together to monitor the human rights record of member states, highlight abuses and make recommendations to improve human rights protection.
- In 2019, Brunei made male homosexual acts punishable by death by stoning. This was immediately condemned by the UN High Commissioner for Human Rights, Michelle Bachelet, as well as by global celebrities such as Elton John and George Clooney. Such negative global publicity led to Brunei quickly suspending the law.
- In 2019, UN Special Rapporteurs were mandated to investigate human rights abuses in Iran, Cambodia, North Korea, Myanmar, Syria and the Palestinian Occupied Territories.
- UN aid agencies, such as the United Nations Children's Fund (UNICEF) and the United Nations High Commission for Refugees, provide emergency support for some of the world's most vulnerable people.
- United Nations peacekeeping missions have played an important role in protecting human rights. In 2019, UN 'blue helmets' were operating in 14 areas, including Haiti, South Sudan and the Democratic Republic of the Congo.

What obstacles does the United Nations face in protecting human rights?

REVISED

- The United Nations' ability to protect human rights is restricted by the ongoing importance of state sovereignty. Human rights law is a form of international soft law which nation-states can ignore.
- The way in which nation-states determine the human rights of their citizens can be in defiance of the Universal Declaration of Human Rights. In 2019, 14 nation-states have the death penalty for homosexuality, and in 16 Muslim-majority countries, converting from Islam to another religion is a crime.
- The United States withdrew from the UN Human Rights Council in 2018, arguing that the Council could not protect human rights when its members included countries which have been condemned for systematic human rights, including China, Saudi Arabia and Algeria.

- In 2019, a United Nations commission of inquiry into the killing of protestors on the Gaza Strip stated that there were 'reasonable grounds to believe that the Israeli Security Forces committed serious violations of human rights and international humanitarian law'. However, Israel responded that its use of military force was legitimate self-defence and that the report was 'hostile, mendacious and slanted'.
- The principles of UN Responsibility to Protect have been ignored in Syria where it is estimated that as many as 400,000 people have died as a result of the conflict.
- The peacekeeping operations of the United Nations have been criticised for not doing enough to protect human rights. UN peacekeepers in Darfur have been hampered by their limited mandate to protect people from Sudanese government forces. In the Democratic Republic of the Congo they have lacked sufficient and trained personnel to effectively intervene to safeguard civilians from warring factions.

Exam tip

The extent to which the United Nations has been successful in combatting climate change is covered more completely in Chapter 6.

Debate

Is the UN making significant progress in addressing environmental issues?

Yes	No
The UN Environment Programme sponsored the Montreal Protocol (1987), which established a global agreement to reduce chlorofluorocarbons (CFCs), so protecting the ozone layer. The General Assembly provides an important forum on which nation-states can debate the potential impact of climate change. Equal voting rights on the General Assembly means that small countries in the developing world which are least likely to be able to cope with climate change have as much influence as powerful nation-states like the United States. United Nations climate change conferences, such as Kyoto (1997) and Paris (2015), have successfully raised global awareness of the importance of confronting the problem of climate change. At the Rio de Janeiro (Earth Summit) in 1992, the United Nations Framework Convention on Climate Change (UNFCCC) established annual conferences at which nation-states come together to discuss how they can resolve the issue of climate change. All member states of the UN have endorsed the UNFCCC. The most far-reaching climate change agreement has been the Paris Treaty (2015). This sets a target of keeping temperature rise well below degree two degrees in the twenty-first century. International condemnation of the Trump administration's actions suggests that the UN has been successful in creating a powerful global consensus that nation-states must work together to reduce carbon emissions. In September 2019 climate change activist Greta Thunberg condemned world leaders for inaction at a UN climate change summit in New York.	As an institution of global governance, the United Nations lacks the supranational authority to effectively enforce compulsory cuts on carbon emissions. This means that the UN can only provide a forum to *encourage* member states to reduce their carbon emissions. At the Paris Conference in 2015 nation-states therefore opposed mandatory cuts on their carbon emissions. Instead they agreed Intended Nationally Determined Contributions (INDCs). As a result, nation-states decide themselves how ambitious their carbon-cutting targets will be. They are also not legally enforceable by the United Nations. In 2019, the UN's Intergovernmental Panel on Climate Change (IPCC) criticised nation-states for not making sufficient progress in reducing carbon emissions. The IPCC warned that if greater efforts were not made, temperature rise could exceed 1.5 degrees within 12 years. The Paris Treaty's ability to resolve the challenge of climate change has also been hampered by the decision of the Trump administration to withdraw from the Treaty since it claims that the cost of the agreed carbon cuts would be too damaging to the US economy. World leaders such as Donald Trump and Jair Bolsonaro of Brazil failed to attend the summit addressed by Thunberg. Their absence demonstrates the UN's inability to compel leading opponents of global climate change to reconsider their views.

How effectively does the United Nations address poverty?

REVISED

- The United Nations provides a constant and powerful message to the world community that poverty must be addressed. The UN has designated 17 October as International Day for the Eradication of Poverty.
- The UN Millennium Development Goals (2000–2015) and the UN **Sustainable Development Goals** (2015–2030) have established globally acknowledged targets for the reduction of poverty.
- UN development agencies also play a significant practical role in combatting poverty.
- The World Health Organization has helped eradicate smallpox and is close to eliminating polio. UNICEF has dramatically reduced childhood deaths through its extensive immunisation programme. The UNDP is coordinating the delivery of the Sustainable Development Goals.
- Classical liberals argue that the free-market reforms of the World Bank and the International Monetary Fund (both of which report to ECOSOC) have been highly significant in reducing poverty. This is because economic globalisation has encouraged greater trade and investment, providing more opportunities for lifting people out of poverty.
- Critics of the United Nations point out that the work of UN development programmes can overlap and that their performance can be poor. ECOSOC is highly bureaucratic and over-staffed, while UN aid agencies, such as UNICEF and the WFP, can end up wasting resources addressing the same problem.
- Aid agencies need to be streamlined and held more accountable for reaching targets. The WHO has been criticised for not dealing more efficiently with the Ebola outbreak in Africa.
- The World Bank and the IMF advancing the principles of globalisation has created greater global wealth than ever before. However, critics claim that it has also created greater inequalities because the profits of global capitalism are shared so unfairly.
- According to **dependency theory**, people in the poorest countries lose out from globalisation because when they engage in free trade they have cheap foreign imports dumped on them. As a result, they have no incentive to industrialise themselves.
- While globalisation encourages rapid industrialisation, it can also reinforce poverty by creating a 'race to the bottom' as companies seek to maximise profits by tolerating poor working conditions.

Sustainable Development Goals are a United Nations initiative which will last from 2015 to 2030. They are 17 interconnected goals focused on eradicating poverty and protecting the planet. They are coordinated by the United Nations Development Programme (UNDP).

Dependency theory is closely connected to world systems theory. It suggests that developing countries are disadvantaged by participating in the liberalisation of global trade. This is because by opening up their markets to the developed world they become dependent on their cheap exports.

Exam tip

Be aware that the UN seeks to reduce poverty through agencies such as the WHO, as well as by encouraging the free-market reforms associated with the World Bank and the IMF. You should therefore connect this chapter with Chapter 4 on global economic governance.

Now test yourself

TESTED

5. Does the evidence suggest the International Court of Justice is a successful or unsuccessful institution of global governance?
6. What are the main ways in which the United Nations tries to protect human rights?
7. Why are the UN's attempts to reduce poverty controversial?
8. In what ways has the UN made progress on combatting climate change and why has it not been able to achieve more?

Answers on p. 107

The North Atlantic Treaty Organization

REVISED

- The **North Atlantic Treaty Organization** was founded in 1949 in the early years of the Cold War. It committed the United States to the defence of western Europe in case of a Soviet attack.
- NATO's key principle is **collective security** (Article 5). This means that an attack on any member will provoke a military response from the whole of NATO. During the Cold War this provided the bedrock of western Europe's defence strategy.
- NATO originally had 12 members. However, since the end of the Cold War in 1991 it has expanded into eastern Europe and by 2019 had 29 members.

North Atlantic Treaty Organization is a military alliance which was established in 1949 to provide the Western democracies with military protection against the Soviet Union. It still provides its members with military defence from external aggression and by 2019 had expanded to 29 members.

Collective security means that an attack on one member state will be regarded as an attack on all member states and so will provoke a collective military response. Article 5 of NATO's constitution commits all its members to the principle of collective security.

To what extent has the role of NATO changed since the end of the Cold War?

- When NATO was established in 1949 its purpose was to protect the Western democracies against potential Soviet aggression. Its role was therefore defensive, and its main area of focus was western Europe.
- When the Soviet Union collapsed in 1991, a much-weakened Russia no longer posed the existential threat it had to western Europe. As a result, NATO seemed to have lost its purpose.
- However, the fall of communism also led to the break-up of Yugoslavia and in the 1990s NATO played an important role trying to bring regional stability to Bosnia and Kosovo. It changed from being a purely defensive alliance to having an important peacemaking and nation-building role.
- The terrorist attacks on New York and Washington DC in 2001 led to Article 5 being activated for the first time in its history. From 2001 to 2014, NATO's International Security Assistance Force (ISAF) was formed to support US operations trying to stabilise Afghanistan. For the first time NATO began to act significantly 'out of area'.
- In 2011, UN Resolution 1973 imposed no-fly zones in Libya in order to protect the civilian population during the revolt against its leader, President Gaddafi. NATO took the principal military role in protecting the civilian population. Controversially, NATO then targeted government forces, leading to the overthrow of the Gaddafi regime.
- In 2018, a NATO mission was established to help train security forces in Iraq in counter-insurgency tactics.
- NATO forces have combatted piracy in the Indian Ocean (Operation Ocean Shield, 2009–2016) and in 2016 Operation Sea Guardian was launched to increase maritime security in the Mediterranean.
- NATO has also been involved in supporting humanitarian missions. For example, it provided emergency relief following the 2005 Pakistan earthquake.
- Between the end of the Cold War and 2019, 13 new eastern European democracies have joined NATO. They could all be vulnerable to possible Russian expansionism and so have been keen to benefit from the protection offered by collective security. This means that NATO still has a strong defensive purpose.
- The annexation of Crimea from Ukraine by Russia in 2014 and Russia's growing military self-confidence have meant that NATO has increasingly returned to its original purpose. Exercises such as Trident

Juncture (2018) have focused on how NATO would respond to a Russian attack on one of its more vulnerable members.

- A major challenge for NATO is having to reach a consensus on the meaning of collective security. Historically, this has meant a traditional military attack on a member state.
- Important new security challenges include cyber attacks on national infrastructures, the targeted use of chemical weapons and outside forces encouraging instability within a member state. Whether or not these sorts of attacks would be enough to trigger Article 5 needs to be clarified if NATO is to retain its effective deterrent capability.

NATO's strengths and weaknesses are presented in Table 3.4.

Typical mistake

It is important when writing about NATO to understand exactly when and where NATO forces have been involved in military operations. Too many students make a mistake in suggesting that the Anglo-American invasion of Iraq in 2003 was a NATO operation.

Table 3.4 NATO: the strengths and weaknesses

Strengths	Weaknesses
Realists argue that NATO is a vital military alliance because of its strong deterrent power.	Critics of NATO argue that its expansion to 29 members has significantly weakened the principle of collective security on which the strength of the alliance is based.
Since 1949, the Soviet Union (and now Russia) has not been prepared to risk activating Article 5 (collective security) by an attack on a member state.	The United States' commitment to NATO is less strong than it has been. In 2018, President Trump did not fully commit to supporting Article 5 if Montenegro was attacked: 'They may get aggressive and congratulations, you're in World War Three.'
As a result, an equilibrium/balance of power has been created in Europe, which has secured peace.	Although they are NATO members, Turkey and Hungary have established stronger political, economic and military links with Russia. This suggests that if there was a conflict with Russia, their commitment to Article 5 might be questioned.
NATO has also maintained a strong political and military bond between the United States and the European democracies. This has been vital in creating a united Western/liberal front against security challenges.	NATO members are supposed to be democracies and NATO encourages the spread of liberal democratic values. However, the governments of Turkey and Hungary have become increasingly autocratic.
NATO's interventions in the Balkans (Bosnia, 1995, and Kosovo, 1999) have deterred aggression and protected civilians. Subsequent nation-building operations by NATO have confronted ethnic and nationalist violence, so securing stability in the Balkans.	NATO's 'out of area' interventions in Afghanistan and Libya have not achieved success. They also showed that some members like the UK were much more prepared to engage in military operations than others.
NATO's expansion into eastern Europe and the Balkans is providing new democracies with protection from potentially being forced back into the Russian sphere of influence.	At the NATO Cardiff Summit (2014), all NATO members agreed to work towards spending 2% of their national budgets on defence. However, only the United States and six European countries reached that target in 2019.
NATO has also shared its military and intelligence expertise with the Iraqi security forces and the African Union (AU). This has helped in nation building, so discouraging conflict.	Germany spent only 1.2% of gross domestic product (GDP) on defence in 2019, although it was the world's fourth biggest economy.
NATO is responding to new security challenges such as piracy, terrorism and the spread of weapons of mass destruction by maintaining maritime surveillance in the Mediterranean.	This imbalance led President Trump to question US commitment to the alliance, especially since the United States is responsible for 70% of NATO's military spending.
In 2014, NATO established a Very High Readiness Joint Task Force to respond to sudden security challenges.	Plans for a European Union army have also challenged NATO'S role as Europe's key defence.
NATO is adapting to new threats such as cyber and chemical attacks and misinformation.	The deterioration of NATO's sense of shared purpose and commitment has undermined the credibility of the alliance.
Russia being accused of backing anti-government forces in eastern Ukraine has also made NATO more open to the possibility that foreign-backed insurgency could trigger Article 5.	

Exam practice

Section A

1 Examine the ways in which the UN Security Council and the UN General Assembly have been criticised. [12]

2 Examine the ways in which the United Nations addresses the issues of human rights enforcement and climate change. [12]

Section C

3 Evaluate the extent to which the United Nations is a successful organisation. [30]

4 Evaluate the extent to which the UN has failed in its peacemaking and peacekeeping role. [30]

5 Evaluate the extent to which the role of NATO has changed in recent years. [30]

6 Evaluate the extent to which NATO is a successful organisation. [30]

Answers and quick quiz 3 online

ONLINE

Summary

You should now have an understanding of the following:

- the main aims of the United Nations
- why the UN Security Council and the UN General Assembly are organised in the way that they are
- how convincing the main criticisms of the UN Security Council and the UN General Assembly are
- the UN's biggest successes and failures in maintaining global peace and security
- the factors undermining the effectiveness of the International Court of Justice
- the effectiveness of the United Nations in encouraging development, promoting human rights and protecting the environment
- the main successes and failures of NATO since its establishment in 1949
- how the role of NATO has changed and developed.

4 Global governance: economic

The significance of the Bretton Woods Conference, 1944

- The World Bank and the International Monetary Fund were established towards the end of the Second World War, in 1944, at the Bretton Woods Conference.
- In preparation for a new post-war world, the World Bank and the IMF would establish a system of global economic governance which would encourage development and ensure international financial stability.
- The IMF would maintain financial exchange rate stability and provide temporary loans to member states suffering from a balance-of-payments crisis. The World Bank would provide long-term loans to nation-states trying to rebuild after the Second World War.
- Both the IMF and the World Bank are associated with neoclassical theories of economic development. This means that they are committed to the principles of the Washington Consensus so that they encourage nation-states to adopt free-trade policies and free-market reforms.
- To some extent the focus of the World Bank and the IMF has changed since their establishment. The World Bank now focuses most of its resources on supporting economic growth in the developing world.
- Since the 1970s, the IMF has not been able to maintain a global fixed rate of exchange. However, the IMF still provides emergency loans to nation-states facing bankruptcy and both remain committed to encouraging economic growth through the adoption of free-market and free-trade reforms.

Neoclassical economic theory and world systems theory

REVISED

The two economic theories are outlined in Table 4.1.

Table 4.1 Neoclassical economic theory and world systems theory

Neoclassical economic theory	World systems theory
According to neoclassical economic theory, the most effective way of achieving development is by a nation-state adopting free-market reforms and engaging in global free trade. By reducing tariffs, removing state control of industry and encouraging private enterprise through lower taxes and privatisation, nation-states benefit from engaging in all the opportunities offered by a global free market. As a result, global development and prosperity are encouraged.	World systems theory is associated with Immanuel Wallerstein (1930–). According to Wallerstein, free trade and free markets enable powerful core states (Global North) to exploit less developed peripheral states (Global South). This is because by encouraging peripheral states in the developing world to open up their markets and commit to free trade, core states in the Global North are able to take advantage of them.

→

Neoclassical economic theory	World systems theory
These free-market principles are rooted in Adam Smith's *The Wealth of Nations* (1776) and in the work of more recent neoliberals such as Friedrich von Hayek (1988–1992) and Milton Friedman (1912–2006). Neoclassical economic development theory provides the theoretical justification for economic globalisation. The IMF and the World Bank are both strongly within classical economic development tradition.	Core states do this by selling peripheral states cheap manufactured products and cheap mass-produced food so that they become 'dependent' on them. Core states also use globalisation to exploit the raw materials and workers of peripheral states so that they can maintain their global economic dominance. This is known as neocolonialism since core states are able to take so much control of the economies of peripheral states that they have a controlling influence over them.

The International Monetary Fund

REVISED

The **International Monetary Fund** works closely with the United Nations Economic and Social Council to ensure global financial stability. It does this in three main ways, as shown in Table 4.2.

Table 4.2 How the IMF ensures global financial stability

Surveillance	The economic policies of member states have to be broadly in tune with the classical economic principles of the IMF. As a result, the IMF can monitor the economic policies of member states and will warn them if they believe that their policies are likely to jeopardise growth and risk damaging their economies.
Lending	If a member state is suffering from a balance-of-payments crisis, it can be impossible for it to access loans from global lenders. In these circumstances the IMF acts as a lender of last resort. These loans will help to stabilise the currency and so restore global confidence in a nation-state, enabling it to recover. In return for the loans, recipient states will be expected to carry out structural adjustment programmes to ensure that the underlying problems which caused the crisis have been resolved.
Technical support	The IMF also offers technical support to member states to help them take advantage of the opportunities offered by a free-market/free-trade economy. This sort of support is open to all member states but is most often accessed by those transitioning to a more liberal economy.

- In 2019, 189 nation-states were members of the IMF. It has approximately $1 trillion at its disposal, which can be loaned to member states experiencing a balance-of-payments crisis. Loans to low-income countries are at 0% interest.
- Member states facing bankruptcy can access emergency loans and this provides an important method of maintaining global economic stability. This is because other nation-states will be reassured that that country can recover, so avoiding a global panic.
- However, the way in which voting is determined on the IMF and its commitment to classical development theory make it a highly controversial organisation.
- Critics claim that the IMF is too dominated by Western interests. Since it is the largest contributor to the IMF, the United States has 16.52% of the vote share on its board of directors. Since 85% of the vote share is needed to reform the IMF's constitution, this gives the United States an effective veto.
- The strong voting influence of European countries like Germany (5.32%), France (4.03%) and the United Kingdom (4.03%) further

The **International Monetary Fund** is a Bretton Woods institution which is committed to global financial stability and economic development. It monitors the economic health of member states, offering technical support and advice and providing loans when members are suffering a balance-of-payments crisis.

contributes to Western dominance of the IMF. This is reflected in the informal tradition that every managing director of the IMF has been a European and every head of the World Bank has been an American citizen.

- As a result, the IMF has been criticised for encouraging free-market/free-trade reforms which, critics claim, serve the interests of Western transnational corporations (TNCs) and may not be appropriate in the developing world.
- The way in which, in return for loans, the IMF requires recipient nation-states to adopt **structural adjustment programmes** (SAPs) is also controversial. This is known as conditionality and means that borrowers have to commit to reforming their economy according to free-market/free-trade principles.
- Critics claim that the requirements of SAPs can be so extensive that their human cost is unacceptable. This is because in order to save a nation-state from bankruptcy, significant cuts in public spending will often be required. The IMF's successes and failures are outlined in Table 4.3.

Structural adjustment programmes refer to loans made by the IMF and the World Bank to nation-states, which are generally conditional upon the recipient government introducing free-market reforms.

Exam tip

Many of the criticisms of the World Bank, the IMF and the WTO connect to criticisms of economic globalisation which are covered in Chapter 2. You should therefore revise both chapters together.

Table 4.3 The IMF: successes and failures

Successes	Failures
IMF emergency loans are vital in restoring confidence in a member state facing a balance-of-payments crisis. This reassures other nation-states that that nation-state will not default on its debts and means that the contagion of economic uncertainty does not spread to other nation-states. The Asian financial crisis (1997–1998) did not spread because countries such as South Korea were quickly saved from bankruptcy by IMF loans. From the start of the global financial crisis in 2008 to 2019, the IMF has provided $325 billion in loans to restore confidence in the global economy to stop the financial panic from spreading. IMF loans to EU states, such as Greece, Ireland and Portugal, during the Eurozone debt crisis (2009) have been vital in restoring confidence in the euro. The significant cuts in public spending (austerity) and free-market reforms which structural adjustment programmes generally require are necessary if the cause of the balance-of-payments crisis is to be resolved. If the loans were unconditional, then similar crises could quickly occur again. Developing countries like India, which have committed to IMF free-market reforms, have best been able to take advantage of globalisation. In 2019, the Indian economy grew by 7.3%. The IMF and the World Bank are both committed to the Heavily Indebted Poor Countries Initiative. This aims to cut the debt of the world's poorest countries so that they can focus their resources on development.	The IMF failed in its work of surveillance when it did not warn member states that their deficits were too high, making them highly vulnerable to a global financial shock. As a result, the collapse of Lehman Brothers in 2008 had a global impact which could have been averted if the IMF had carried out its work of surveillance better. The legitimacy of the IMF in the developing world is undermined by the fact that its 11 managing directors have all been European. Christine Lagarde (2011–), for example, is the fifth French head of the IMF. According to the economist Joseph Stiglitz, the IMF reflects 'the interests and ideology of the western financial community'. The public spending cuts and free-market reforms which SAPs require (privatisation, high interest rates, trade liberalisation) are highly controversial. This is because such 'shock therapy' can damage an already weak economy. The human cost of austerity can also be unacceptable. High unemployment levels and cuts in public spending harm those most dependent on welfare support. Stiglitz has also criticised 'the one size fits all' approach of the IMF, arguing that the principles of economic liberalism do not take into account the diverse needs of nation-states at different stages of development. As a result, some indebted countries are now trying to access loans which do not require conditionality. In 2018, Pakistan applied to Saudi Arabia for financial support before turning to the IMF.

The World Bank

REVISED

- Whereas the IMF is focused on providing short-term loans to nation-states facing a balance-of-payments crisis, the **World Bank** concentrates on long-term development.
- As on the IMF, voting on the World Bank favours Western powers, with the United States having 17.25% of the vote share.
- By tradition the president of the World Bank is also an American citizen, so the World Bank is firmly associated with Western-orientated theories of economic development.
- The World Bank makes loans to middle-income countries through its International Bank for Reconstruction and Development (IBRD). Loans to the poorest nations in the world are made by the World Bank through its International Development Agency (IDA).
- World Bank loans require no, or very low, interest repayments. In return for the loans, recipient nation-states are usually expected to introduce free-market structural adjustment programmes.
- According to the World Bank, the adoption of free-market reforms provides the most effective way of achieving higher levels of economic growth in the developing world. However, critics of the World Bank argue that these reforms encourage **neocolonial dependency**.
- As well as being committed to free-market reforms, the World Bank has specialist knowledge in a range of development policies.
- As a result, World Bank development programmes have a strong human and environmental focus. These include cutting carbon emissions, encouraging gender equality, improving education and social cohesion, and combatting infectious diseases such as AIDS, malaria and tuberculosis.
- The World Bank is focused on quantifiable results and so its principle of 'achievement by country' (ABC) is central to all of its development work. Its successes and failures are outlined in Table 4.4.

The **World Bank** is a Bretton Woods institution which provides advice on development and offers long-term, low-interest loans to developing countries. It is committed to ending extreme poverty and supports development programmes throughout the developing world.

Neocolonial dependency – Marxist critics of economic globalisation argue that it enables developed nation-states to exploit the raw materials and workforces of the developing world. The way in which the developing world becomes economically dependent on the developed world amounts to a form of colonialism.

Table 4.4 The World Bank: successes and failures

Successes	Failures
World Bank structural adjustment programmes have encouraged developing countries to focus on production areas in which they have a natural advantage. Structural adjustment programmes in Ghana have encouraged farmers to move from inefficient rice production to the export of bananas, cocoa and pineapples. Rwanda is gaining foreign capital through 'gorilla tourism'. Ethiopia is being given technical support to grow its export market in footwear. World Bank free-market reform projects have encouraged India to take advantage of new opportunities in global trade. This has led to India rising from a low-income to a low-middle-income country.	Given the voting influence of the United States on the World Bank, the US President is effectively able to select the president of the World Bank. This means that the focus of the World Bank is likely to be closely aligned to US economic strategy. In 2019, President Trump nominated a close ally, David Malpass, to succeed Jim Kim as World Bank president. A main criticism of the World Bank is that it is too focused on free-market structural adjustment programmes. Critics argue that the transformation to free markets and free trade can hurt the poorest people in the developing world. This is because they lose job security when markets are liberalised. The resulting unemployment can lead to acute social problems.

Successes	Failures
The World Bank has also been responsible for major infrastructure projects in the developing world. Between 2011 and 2018, the IDA, which works in the poorest parts of the world, financed the immunisation of 274 million children and provided better clean water access for 86 million.	From 2004 to 2013, structural adjustment programmes led to 3.4 million people being 'involuntarily resettled'.
The World Bank's gender equality strategy means that its development projects encourage female education and enhance female opportunities in the workplace. In sub-Saharan Africa, girls attending primary school rose from 76.1% in 2000 to 95% in 2017.	The way in which loans are conditional on developing countries adopting free-market reforms challenges their sovereignty. It also forces them to adopt free-market policies which may not be appropriate to their stage of development.
Since the impact of climate change is going to be felt most immediately on the poorest people in the world, the World Bank is at the forefront of efforts to deal with the threat. From 2013 to 2017, the IDA annually committed $2 billion to help poor countries adapt to climate change and $1.7 billion to mitigate its impact.	Ha-Joon Chang (1963–) in *Kicking Away the Ladder* (2002) argues that if developing countries adopt free-market reforms too soon, they will not be able to protect themselves from becoming peripheral states trapped in neocolonial dependency.
All IDA projects incorporate ways of better protecting the environment. For example, by harnessing renewable energy, improving crop yields with less water.	This is because their economies will be swamped by cheap mass-produced exports which they become dependent upon. There is a good case for developing countries to protect and subsidise their economies until they are powerful enough to compete more fairly with core states.
The World Bank has also encouraged debt relief for the world's poorest countries through the Heavily Indebted Poor Countries Initiative.	The way in which the World Bank encourages the export of 'cash crops' by developing countries means that they remain in a state of neocolonial dependency since prices are generally set by transnational corporations.
Since corrupt and inefficient central government is a major cause of poverty, World Bank development projects often focus on lending directly to local communities. This is known as community-driven development (CDD). From 2010 to 2015, the IDA completed 90 projects responsible for 164,000 local projects reaching 176 million people. These projects encourage initiative, transparency, accountability and business self-confidence among local communities.	Free-market reforms often require dramatic cuts in public spending in order to stabilise a currency to attract foreign investment. However, these reforms will hurt the poorest people in society. China being the second biggest recipient of World Bank loans is controversial given that it is the world's second biggest economy (2019).

Typical mistake

Since they are all associated with economic liberalism, students can confuse the World Bank, the IMF and the WTO. It is therefore important that you precisely understand the different purposes and functions of each of these Bretton Woods institutions.

Exam tip

To give your writing conviction, research recent examples of World Bank and IMF successes and failures.

Now test yourself

TESTED

1. What is the connection between the International Monetary Fund, the World Bank and classical economic theory? Why is this controversial?
2. What are the main principles of world systems theory?
3. Provide examples of IMF/World Bank structural adjustment programmes which have been damaging/successful.
4. What have been the most successful development programmes of the World Bank in recent years?

Answers on p. 107

The World Trade Organization

REVISED

- The **World Trade Organization** was established in 1995 to encourage free trade between nation-states. It is the successor to the General Agreement on Trade and Tariffs (GATT), which was created in 1948.
- Its 164 members (2019) account for 98% of world trade. The ministerial conference is the WTO's highest executive body and meets every two years.
- The WTO's commitment to free trade is based on the liberal principle that free trade encourages global prosperity and discourages nationalism and conflict. It is one of the Bretton Woods institutions of global economic governance.
- Members of the WTO negotiate on the principle of 'most favoured nation'. This means that a member state cannot grant special trading rights to another without granting them to all members of the WTO. According to WTO rules, all members of the organisation should equally engage in free trade with each other.
- The WTO focuses on particular areas where trade can be liberalised during successive trade rounds. The Doha Round began in 2001 and tried to open up markets in the developed world to goods from the developing world.
- The rise of protectionism in the United States during the Trump administration has posed a huge challenge for the free-trade principles of the WTO. In 2018, the Director-General of the WTO, Roberto Azevedo, said that world trade was facing its 'worst crisis' since 1947. The WTO's successes and failures are presented in Table 4.5.

The **World Trade Organization** was created in 1995 to arbitrate trade disputes between member states and encourage them to liberalise trade by reducing tariffs and subsidies.

Table 4.5 The WTO: successes and failures

Successes	Failures
By negotiating the global liberalisation of trade, GATT/WTO has helped to boost exports. World exports in 2016 were 250 times higher than they were in 1948.	The democratic rules of the WTO can mean that it can be difficult to reach decisions. This is because member states will only agree to trade deals which they see as being in their interests.
The WTO has steadily expanded its membership from 124 nation-states (1995) to 164 (2019). These include China (2001) and Russia (2012).	To be successful the WTO requires its membership to be fully committed to the principles of trade liberalisation. This is not always the case.
The expansion of the WTO has been responsible for encouraging dialogue and connections between countries, so reducing the risk of conflict.	The unwillingness of the United States, Japan and the European Union to open their markets to agricultural products from the developing world led to the failure of the Doha Round of trade negotiations.
The Uruguay Round (1986–1994) liberalised trade in intellectual property, telecommunications and banking. This was important because previous rounds had focused only on industrial products.	Member states can self-categorise themselves as developing states. China, India and Brazil do this, giving them longer to reduce tariffs and subsidies. This has undermined the confidence of developed countries in the WTO.
In 2013, at the Bali ministerial conference, WTO members negotiated the Agreement on Trade Facilitation, which is designed to increase global trade by reducing border administration which has generally been most slow and costly in developing countries.	Although world trade has increased dramatically, the advantages of economic growth have not been shared equally. This has led to an anti-globalisation backlash, which has further challenged the ability of the WTO to reach consensus.
From 2005 to 2019 the WTO's Aid for Trade programme provided $340 billion in support to the developing world so that it can more fully participate in global trade.	As the world's biggest economy, the protectionist policies of the Trump administration have further undermined the WTO's credibility.

➜

Successes	Failures
The WTO's Appellate Body has resolved a number of trade disputes which could have escalated into trade wars. In 2015, China agreed to stop restricting the export of rare earth metals when it lost a case brought by the United States, Japan and the European Union. This was a significant case given the importance of rare earth metals in modern technology such as hybrid cars and wind turbines. Since 2005, the WTO has been arbitrating a dispute over whether the EU has illegally subsidised Airbus and the United States acted in the same way with Boeing. Both sides have acknowledged that they would prefer the WTO to resolve the dispute rather than having to resort to retaliatory tariffs.	The WTO has failed to stop the outbreak of a major trade war between the United States and China. From 2017 to 2019, the Trump administration imposed $250 billion of tariffs on Chinese goods. In response, China placed $110 billion worth of tariffs on US goods. The WTO has been criticised for favouring powerful lobbying interests. In 2001, the United States brought a successful case at the WTO demanding that the EU stop granting preferential access to small banana traders in the developing world. The main beneficiary of the judgment was the US banana producer Chiquita, which has huge plantations in South America. The WTO fails to protect workers' rights which can be harmed by industrialisation. The WTO also does not take responsibility for the way in which the expansion of trade damages the environment.

Exam tip

Independent research of the main organs of economic global governance will give your writing greater maturity. When you research the WTO, discover why the sea turtle is often seen as emblematic of its failure to protect the environment.

The Group of Seven

REVISED

- The **Group of Seven** is an organ of global governance. G7 members represent the largest advanced economies in the world. These comprise the United States, Canada, the United Kingdom, France, Germany, Italy and Japan.
- The EU is a regular participant and non-governmental and intergovernmental institutions can be invited to join the discussions.
- Russia was a member from 1997 to 2014 when it was known as the G8. Following its suspension in 2014 as a result of the annexation of Crimea, the group reverted to the G7.
- The leaders of the G7 meet annually at summit meetings. By sharing ideas and building trust and cooperation they aim to establish a unified approach by the world's most developed countries to global issues such as trade, climate change and security.
- The G7 has been criticised for perpetuating the North/South divide since only advanced economies attend its meetings.
- The G7 also lacks coercive power and depends upon its leaders agreeing to a shared approach to collective dilemmas. This means that its influence is limited since it has no supranational control over its members.
- The communiqués which the G7 publishes at the end of its meetings are statements of intent and so have no binding influence.
- In spite of this, the G7 has achieved some successes. In 2005 at the Gleneagles summit it was agreed to write off the $40 billion debt owed by 18 heavily indebted poor countries. In 2015 at the Schloss Elmau summit the leaders agreed the Global Apollo Programme to combat climate change by encouraging the generation of carbon-free electricity.

The **Group of Seven** (G7) is a group of the seven strongest economies in the developed world. Meetings take place between their leaders every year to try to achieve a collective approach to global problems.

- However, the 'America first' strategy of the Trump presidency demonstrates how limited the G7 is if its members fail to work together.
- At the G7 Quebec summit (2018) the developing trade war between the United States and Canada and the EU could not be resolved. The United States also failed to agree to implement the Paris Climate change accords.
- The United States' request that Russia be readmitted to membership (after its suspension following the annexation of Crimea in 2014) was rejected by the other six. President Trump then failed to endorse the traditional communiqué at the end of the Quebec summit.
- The G7 Biarritz summit (2019) confirmed sharp differences between President Macron and President Trump over how the world community should respond to Brazil's forest fires.
- However, a meeting between President Macron and the Iranian foreign minister, Javad Zarif, on the sidelines of the Biarritz summit shows how global focus on G7 meetings can encourage potential diplomatic breakthroughs.

The Group of Twenty

REVISED

- The **Group of Twenty** was established to reflect the changing balance of global economic power. Its membership therefore comprises the 19 biggest economies in the developed *and* the developing world as well as the European Union, representing 85% of the world economy.
- Like the G7, the G20 holds annual summits which NGOs and IGOs are invited to attend. The focus of the G20 is primarily economic, social and environmental issues. At the end of each conference a joint communiqué is issued.
- Like the G7, the G20 lacks binding power and so some critics have dismissed its meetings as irrelevant.
- However, the London Conference (2009) provided a strong international response to the global economic crisis. Members pledged $1.1 trillion to restore faith in the global economy and the Financial Stability Board was set up. This reports on the economies of the G20 and recommends policies designed to avert another financial crash.
- The decline of internationalism and the new assertiveness of nationalist leaders such as Vladimir Putin, Donald Trump and Xi Jinping has made it more difficult to achieve agreement at the G20.
- However, it could be argued that this has made the G20 more important as a regular point of contact for world leaders.
- The G20 conference in Buenos Aires (2018), for example, provided an opportunity for President Trump and President Xi Jinping to discuss their trade war. Western leaders were also able to raise the murder of the journalist Jamal Khashoggi with the Saudi crown prince, Mohammed bin Salman.

The **Group of Twenty** (G20) represents the biggest economies in the world in both the developed and the developing worlds. Like the G7, its leaders meet annually to discuss how best to respond to pressing global issues.

Typical mistake

Students often fail to revise the G7 and G20 because their role and purpose can seem less readily apparent than the Bretton Woods institutions. It is therefore very important that you revise these institutions thoroughly. Update yourself by making notes on the significance of their most recent meetings.

Now test yourself

TESTED

5 What are the aims of the World Trade Organization and how well does it achieve them?
6 What are the main criticisms of the WTO?
7 What are the aims of the G7 and how well does it achieve them?
8 What are the aims of the G20 and how well does it achieve them?

Answers on p. 108

What is poverty and what causes it?

REVISED

- The World Bank defines extreme poverty, in income terms, as living on a wage of less than $1.90 a day. According to the United Nations (1995), extreme poverty is 'a condition characterised by severe deprivation of basic human needs including food, safe drinking water, sanitation facilities, health, shelter, education and information'.
- In 2018, the World Bank estimated that 8.6% of the world's population live in extreme poverty.
- The causes of poverty are controversial. According to dependency theory, structural adjustment programmes and trade liberalisation have been major causes of poverty in the developing world.
- Neoclassical economists respond that trade liberalisation actually provides people with a way out of poverty by opening up new business opportunities. Tariffs and subsidies, on the other hand, protect producers from competition, enabling them to increase prices for consumers. They also discourage the need for enterprise and innovation.
- It has been suggested that corrupt, inefficient and protectionist governments in the developing world are the main reason for poverty since they discourage business initiative.

The difference between the orthodox and alternative models of development

REVISED

- Since poverty has traditionally been seen in terms of wage levels, the orthodox model of development emphasises economic growth as the surest measure of development.
- The Bretton Woods institutions therefore have generally measured success in terms of economic growth.
- However, economic development can create its own problems. Industrialisation can lead to 'a race to the bottom' in squalid factories and greater carbon emissions which contribute to climate change.
- Therefore, the alternative model of development focuses on other non-material measures of development which can contribute just as much as economic growth to human wellbeing. Amartya Sen's *Development as Freedom* (1999) provides a classic statement of the alternative approach to development.
- The alternative model of development measures development in a more social way, emphasising the extent to which it improves quality of life and does not damage the environment.
- According to the alternative measure, development should also encourage political freedom and the opportunity for self-realisation.
- Development projects should empower women so that they can contribute to the workforce and have greater control over their lives.
- The alternative measure of development is also committed to sustainability so that the resources of the planet are not jeopardised for future generations.
- Faster growth rates can lead to a less equal and more polarised society and so development should encourage social cohesion and seek to integrate communities.

The North/South divide

REVISED

- The Brandt Reports (1980/1983) first used the term **North/South divide** to describe the differences between the developed and the developing worlds.
- The Global North is developed, which means that its economy is industrialised. Investment and aid flow from the Global North to the Global South and most transnational corporations are based there.
- The Global North has structural dominance of the main organs of global economic governance, e.g. the World Bank, the IMF and the WTO.
- The Global North is more likely to have stable democratic forms of government and to respect individual human rights.
- According to the Brandt Reports, the Global South is more focused on the production of food and the export of raw materials.
- Life expectancy is lower in the Global South due to infectious diseases. Governments are more **autocratic**, less stable and more corrupt.

North/South divide is a term coined by the Brandt Report. It contrasts the poverty of the less developed agricultural Global South with the prosperity of the more industrialised and developed Global North.

An **autocratic state** is a nation-state in which one individual has absolute control. There are no limits on the actions that individual can take. The government can claim no popular legitimacy and the rule of law does not exist.

Debate

Is the North/South divide still a meaningful term?

Yes	No
According to world systems theory, the North/South divide has been reinforced by neoclassical economic theory. This is because the developing world has been pressured into opening up its markets by the Bretton Woods institutions. As a result, the Global South has been swamped by cheap exports from the Global North and so has not been able to achieve a first stage of industrialisation. This has ensured that the Global North has been able to maintain neocolonial control of the Global South. Transnational corporations exploit workers in factories in the developing world and the focus of the Global South on the export of primary materials means that it remains subservient to the interests of the Global North. The way in which the Global North extracts raw materials from the Global South means that its prosperity is often dependent upon global commodity prices. Africa's share of global trade decreased from 2.8% in 2013 to 2.3% in 2017 because of its reliance on the sale of raw materials. Extreme poverty is still most concentrated in the Global South. In 2019, of the 736 million people living in extreme poverty, 413 million were in Sub-Saharan Africa.	Neoclassical supporters of economic globalisation/the Washington Consensus argue that it has led to unprecedented economic growth in the developing world. This has led to growing convergence between the Global North and the Global South. The way in which the G20 now rivals the influence of the G7 is a good example of this. By engaging in trade liberalisation through opening up its markets, China has become the second biggest economy in the world. The World Bank estimates that since 1978, and the beginning of trade liberalisation, 850 million Chinese citizens have been lifted out of poverty. As a result of economic globalisation, the Global North is now losing jobs to the Global South. This is why the Trump administration has been so protectionist and renegotiated the North American Free Trade Agreement in 2018. In 2019, many of the fastest growing economies in the world were in Sub-Saharan Africa, led by Ethiopia (7.9%) and Rwanda (7.6%). The growth rate in Bangladesh in 2019 was 7.4% and in India it was 7.3%. Critics of the North/South divide also point out that some nation-states in the Global North share characteristics of the Global South. Russia, for example, is a major exporter of raw materials and has a poor record on democracy.

Typical mistake

Since economic globalisation is such a highly emotive issue, some students may be tempted to write one-sided essays. It is very important that they are fair and balanced in order to ensure high marks on assessment objectives A02 and A03.

Debate

Is neocolonialism the main cause of poverty in the developing world?

Yes	No
According to world systems/dependency theory, trade liberalisation enables core states in the Global North to maintain neocolonial control over peripheral states in the Global South.	Trade liberalisation has encouraged dramatic growth in the Global South. This is because the developing world has been able to utilise its cheap workforce to achieve industrialisation.
Core states do this by dumping cheap manufactured products and cheaply produced mass food on peripheral states. By becoming dependent on them they fail to develop themselves.	Economic globalisation also drives down the price of food and consumer goods, increasing the buying power of wages. The decline of extreme poverty has been due to the developing world engaging in globalisation.
The Global South is encouraged to export raw materials. Its cheap workforce is exploited in the factories of transnational corporations whose shareholders then accumulate most of the profits.	China, although still a developing country, has taken advantage of trade liberalisation to lift millions out of poverty.
The Global North maintains its neocolonial control through its influence on the World Bank and the IMF. SAPs undermine job security and cut public services. This mostly affects the poorest in society.	Poverty in the Global South is caused by other factors. In particular, corrupt governments undermine business confidence and deter overseas investment. Some of the poorest countries in the world (Burundi, Central African Republic, Haiti) have the worst record on good governance and a history of conflict.
The WTO Doha trade round has failed because the Global North has refused to open its markets to agricultural products from the developing world. This shows how the Global North uses its structural power to keep the Global South in a dependent status.	Land-locked countries with poor natural resources (Central African Republic, Niger) are least able to take advantage of trade liberalisation.

NGOs, poverty and development

REVISED

- **Non-governmental organisations**, such as Oxfam, Save the Children and Christian Aid, are important in ensuring that the issue of global poverty is not ignored.
- The reports they publish keep pressure on governments to address poverty. Oxfam is monitoring the effectiveness of the Sustainable Development Goals (2015–2030). Christian Aid is putting pressure on the World Bank to fully commit to sustainable and renewable energy in its Big Shift campaign.
- Save the Children's 'Ambition for Children 2030' aims to ensure that no child dies of preventable diseases by then. *Médecins sans Frontières* (Doctors without Borders) specialises in providing aid in conflict zones.

Non-governmental organisations (NGOs) are non-profit organisations which work with governments, regional organisations and intergovernmental organisations to achieve their social, political and environmental objectives.

- The Gates Foundation is a global leader in the fight against AIDS, tuberculosis and malaria. The Carter Foundation has virtually eradicated guinea worm. In 1986, there were 3.5 million reported cases of guinea worm; in 2018 there were just 28.
- However, critics of NGOs argue that they can be responsible for a 'white saviour complex', which means that governments in the developing world do not have to take responsibility for their own citizens.
- Dambisa Moyo has criticised international aid in *Dead Aid* (2009), arguing that the good intentions of NGOs stifle enterprise in the developing world and allow corrupt and inefficient governments not to be held accountable for their failures.

Now test yourself

TESTED

9 What is the North/South divide and why is it a contested term?
10 What is neocolonialism and how has it been accused of increasing poverty?
11 What are the different measures of development?
12 In what ways has the developing world been accused of being responsible for poverty?

Answers on p. 108

Exam practice

Section A

1 Explain the conflict between classical economic theory and world systems theory. [12]
2 Explain the differences between the orthodox and alternative models of economic development. [12]

Section C

3 Evaluate the extent to which the World Bank and the International Monetary Fund can be viewed as successful organisations. [30]
4 Evaluate the extent to which the North/South divide is still a meaningful term. [30]
5 Evaluate the extent to which the World Trade Organization is a failed institution. [30]
6 Evaluate the extent to which the main institutions of global economic governance are effective at encouraging economic growth and maintaining economic stability. [30]

Answers and quick quiz 4 online

ONLINE

Summary

You should now have an understanding of the following:

- the main purposes and functions of the World Bank and the International Monetary Fund
- why there is so much tension between classical economic development theory and world systems theory
- what neocolonialism is and why it is such a controversial term
- the various ways in which poverty and development can be measured and why that is significant
- the term 'North/South divide' and the extent to which it is still relevant
- why the World Trade Organization was established and the extent to which it has achieved its objectives
- the purpose of the G7 and the G20 and to what extent they are significant
- how effective non-governmental organisations are in combatting global poverty.

5 Global governance: human rights

Origins of international law

International law provides a way of bringing order and stability into global politics. Although international relations are anarchic because there is no supranational authority to which all nation-states are equally accountable, nation-states usually accept certain standards of international behaviour. For example:

- Diplomatic immunity from arrest is a globally accepted privilege which represents a good example of international customary law. This means that the law protecting diplomats is not written down but it is still globally acknowledged.
- The way in which nation-states agree to the terms of treaties is another example of international law in operation.

International law is law that all nation-states and other international actors are expected to obey in their relations with each other.

Post-1945 development of international law and institutions

REVISED

- The Second World War provided a huge spur to the development of international law. The way in which Nazi and Japanese aggression had flouted international standards of behaviour, together with the implementation of genocide and systematic human rights abuses, led to a rapid expansion of the meaning and scope of international law.
- The Charter of the United Nations (1945) established that there are only two instances when nation-states can use force against other nation-states. These are self-defence (Article 51) or as part of a United Nations peace-enforcement operation (Article 42).
- In 1945 the International Court of Justice (ICJ, World Court) was established. The ICJ is the judicial arm of the United Nations and its 15 judges attempt to settle disputes between the member states of the United Nations.
- At the trial of leading Nazis before the Nuremberg War Crimes Tribunal (1945–1946) the legal principle of 'crimes against humanity' was first used as a legal basis for prosecution.
- Nuremberg also established the legal principle of 'crimes against peace', enabling the prosecution of individuals for 'waging a war of aggression or conspiring to do so'.
- In 1948 the Universal Declaration of Human Rights was adopted by the United Nations General Assembly. This document provides the most important statement of the rights which all human beings can claim.
- The European Convention on Human Rights was signed in 1950. The 47 member states of the Council of Europe are signatories to the Convention. Cases can be brought to the European Court of Human Rights in Strasbourg if a member state is alleged to have acted against the Convention.

Post-1991 development of international law and institutions

REVISED

- The ending of the Cold War in the period 1989–1991 provided another boost to the development of international human rights-based law. Now that international relations were no longer defined by the bipolar conflict between the United States and the Soviet Union, the protection of **universal human rights** gained new prominence.
- The Office of United Nations High Commissioner for Human Rights was created in 1993. The role of the UN High Commissioner for Human Rights (Michelle Bachelet 2018–) is to protect and promote human rights enforcement.
- In 1993 the United Nations tribunal for the former Yugoslavia was established to try crimes committed during the break-up of Yugoslavia. This was the first **international tribunal** since the end of the Second World War. It was followed by tribunals to prosecute human rights abuses which had taken place in Cambodia, Rwanda and Sierra Leone.
- These tribunals laid the foundations for the creation of the International Criminal Court in 2002. The ICC prosecutes individuals for genocide, crimes against humanity and war crimes if national courts are unable or unprepared to provide justice. Its main functions are presented in Table 5.1 together with those of the ICJ.

Universal human rights refer to the permanent rights which all human beings can claim equally, regardless of sex, religion or culture. These rights are based on our membership of the human race and should not be restricted in any way.

International tribunals are judicial bodies set up in cooperation with the United Nations to try individuals in specific nation-states for war crimes, crimes against humanity and genocide.

Exam tip

When writing about the protection of human rights by international law, clearly place this within a liberal context.

Table 5.1 The ICJ and the ICC: main functions

International Court of Justice	International Criminal Court
The International Court of Justice was established by the United Nations Charter in 1945.	The International Criminal Court was established in 2002 by the Rome Statute.
The ICJ sits permanently in The Hague. Its 15 judges are selected by the UN General Assembly and the Security Council.	Nation-states which accept the Rome Statute become members of the ICC and accept its jurisdiction.
The ICJ delivers judgments on cases involving nation-states. These rulings can be enforced by the UN Security Council.	The ICC is in permanent session in The Hague. The chief prosecutor of the ICC decides which cases will be investigated.
The ICJ can also provide non-binding advisory opinions to United Nations agencies and bodies.	The ICC prosecutes individuals for the international crimes of genocide, war crimes and crimes against humanity if justice cannot be achieved in national courts.

Why is it difficult to enforce international human rights law?

REVISED

Nation-state sovereignty

- International human rights law is an example of a liberal approach to global politics. This is because it is founded on the principle that the global community has a moral obligation to protect the human rights of all people.
- However, this is difficult to enforce because nation-states value their sovereignty and can choose not to comply with human rights-based

international law. The Charter of the United Nations recognises state sovereignty as the basis of international relations when it states that 'the organisation is based on the principle of the sovereign equality of all its members'.

- The problem of enforcing human rights-based law provides a good example of the conflict between the good intentions of liberalism and a realist emphasis on the importance of state sovereignty.
- As a result, international human rights law can be seen as 'soft' rather than 'hard' law. This means that although it has significant moral force, nation-states can still act in defiance of it. If they do so there is generally little that can be done to enforce compliance.
- International courts, such as the International Court of Justice, the International Criminal Court and the European Court of Human Rights, find it difficult to enforce their rulings if nation-states refuse to cooperate with them.
- President Trump's national security adviser, John Bolton, has attacked the ICC as a threat to American interests. According to Bolton, 'We will let the ICC die on its own. After all, for all intents and purposes, the ICC is already dead to us.'

Exam tip

Revise human rights at the same time as the nation-state and national sovereignty. A good understanding of the significance of national sovereignty is important in appreciating the limits of international law.

Powerful states are unaccountable for their actions

- The successful implementation of international law requires all nation-states to be equally accountable for their actions.
- However, powerful nation-states can avoid taking responsibility for human rights infringements. The United States, for example, is unlikely to be prosecuted for alleged human rights abuses such as water-boarding.
- The United States' insistence that the former Iraqi dictator, Saddam Hussein, be tried by an Iraqi court rather than a United Nations tribunal further demonstrates how international law is not impartially implemented.
- Russia has also not been held accountable for alleged human rights violations in the Syrian civil war.
- China is able to ignore international criticism of her extensive use of the death penalty and restrictions of religious, social and political freedoms.
- As powerful nation-states can dismiss international criticism, this undermines international standards of human rights enforcement. According to the radical political philosopher and activist Noam Chomsky, 'For the powerful crimes are those that others commit.'

How effective are international courts and tribunals in enforcing human rights law?

- The purpose of international courts and tribunals is to punish those who abuse human rights and to act as a deterrent against further human rights violations.
- All of them have achieved significant successes which have helped to develop the principle of international human law. However, the effectiveness of the **International Criminal Court** and the **International Court of Justice** is undermined by state sovereignty.
- The ICC has also been accused of political bias and the tribunals have been criticised for representing victors' justice. Its successes and failures are outlined in Table 5.3, while Table 5.2 addresses those of the ICJ.

The **International Criminal Court** was created by the Rome Statute in 2002. The Court sits in The Hague and prosecutes individuals accused of war crimes, crimes against humanity and genocide.

The **International Court of Justice** was established in 1945. It is the main judicial body of the United Nations. It sits permanently in The Hague and delivers judgments and advisory opinions in cases involving the actions of nation-states.

Table 5.2 The ICJ: successes and failures

Failures	Successes
All 193 member states of the United Nations are members of the ICJ. However, only 73 of them have agreed *in advance* to be bound by the judgments of the court. This shows how unwilling nation-states are to accept supranational judicial limitations on their sovereignty. The following cases demonstrate the way in which ICJ judgments can be ignored. In 1979, Iran refused to acknowledge the jurisdiction of the ICJ when the United States brought a case against it for the seizure of the US embassy in Tehran. In 1984, the United States withdrew from the compulsory jurisdiction of the ICJ when it was found guilty of trying to illegally overthrow the government of Nicaragua. In 2004, Israel reacted angrily to an advisory opinion by the ICJ that the wall Israel had built to separate it from the Palestinian territories was illegal. In 2018, Iran brought a case to the ICJ arguing that the re-imposition of sanctions by the Trump administration was illegal. Although the ICJ 'reprimanded' the United States and ordered it 'to lift restrictive measures', the Trump administration ignored the judgment. The UN Security Council can enforce the judgments of the ICJ. However, this has never occurred. Divisions on the Security Council between the permanent five also make it unlikely that this will ever occur.	The ICJ is important because it is a permanent body of the United Nations which holds nation-states accountable for breaches of international law. Although it lacks an effective way of enforcing its judgments, the ICJ possesses great moral authority. Nation-states therefore often accept its judgments. In 1992, the ICJ resolved a border dispute between El Salvador and Honduras. In 2002, the ICJ resolved a border dispute between Nigeria and Cameroon. In 1988, Iran Air Flight 655 was mistakenly shot down by the USS Vincennes, killing all 290 on board. In 1996, the governments of the United States and Iran reached a settlement at the ICJ. Although the United States did not accept legal liability it did pay compensation to the victims' families and expressed 'deep regret over the loss of lives caused by the incident'. In 2009, Belgium brought a case to the ICJ demanding that Senegal begin the trial of former President of Chad, Hissène Habré, for crimes against humanity. Belgium won the case and Senegal put Habré on trial.

Exam tip

You will explain the limitations on human rights-based international law best if you can place it within the context of a realist approach to global politics.

Table 5.3 The ICC: successes and failures

Failures	Successes
Three members of the UN Security Council (the United States, Russia and China) do not recognise its jurisdiction. 70% of the world's population is outside the jurisdiction of the ICC. The ICC has no enforcement powers and has to rely on nation-states to cooperate with it. The ICC's prosecution of President Uhuru Kenyatta of Kenya was dropped because Kenya refused to cooperate. Although indicted by the ICC, President Omar al-Bashir of Sudan continued to travel across Africa.	Since its establishment in 2002, 64% of the nation-states in the United Nations have ratified the Rome Statute and so accept the authority of the ICC. This is a major step forward in establishing the principle that international standards of justice can be applied *within* nation-states. This directly challenges the Westphalian principle of state sovereignty that nation-states possess absolute sovereignty within their borders. The ICC represents the principle that nation-states are all equally accountable to the rule of law.

→

Failures	Successes
In 2018, the conviction of Jean-Pierre Bemba, the former vice-president of the Democratic Republic of the Congo, was overturned. Bemba was the most senior politician to be convicted by the ICC and his release has significantly undermined its credibility. In 2019, the case against the former president of Côte d'Ivoire, Laurent Gbagbo, for organising post-election violence, was dropped because of insufficient evidence. Amnesty International has called this 'a crushing disappointment'. Since only Africans (2002–2019) have been indicted by the ICC, it has been accused of having a post-colonial bias. President Kenyatta of Kenya has called the ICC 'a toy of declining imperialist powers'.	The Office of Chief Prosecutor is able to initiate cases. This makes the ICC more proactive than the ICJ, which has to wait for cases to come to it. Since it is a permanent court, the ICC provides an ever-present reminder that the international community has a responsibility to protect the rights of citizens if they are not protected by nation-states. The ICC has convicted Thomas Lubanga (14 years) and Germain Katanga (12 years) for crimes committed during the Congolese civil war. Although by 2019 it had only prosecuted Africans, the ICC has opened investigations into human rights abuses committed across the world.

Typical mistake

Students can confuse the purpose and functions of the International Criminal Court and the International Court of Justice. It is therefore important that you have a clear understanding of their different responsibilities.

Exam tip

Keep up to date with cases being heard by the ICJ and the ICC. This will give your writing real conviction and maturity.

Now test yourself

TESTED

1. What is the International Court of Justice and what factors undermine its effectiveness?
2. What is the International Criminal Court and what factors undermine its effectiveness?
3. What have been the most significant successes and failures of the ICJ?
4. What have been the most significant successes and failures of the ICC?

Answers on p. 108

The European Court of Human Rights

REVISED

The European Court of Human Rights is responsible for upholding the European Convention on Human Rights. Its influence has been important in developing widely accepted standards of human rights protection across Europe.

- In 1982, Northern Ireland legalised homosexual acts after legislation making it a criminal activity was condemned by the European Court of Human Rights. The way in which the Court requires all members of the Council of Europe to protect the rights of lesbian, gay, bisexual and transgender (LGBT) people provides a strong moral framework for their defence.
- In a number of cases, including Leyla Şahin v. Turkey (2004), the European Court of Human Rights has stated that restrictions on the wearing of religious symbols and clothing is legal.

However, like the ICJ and the ICC, the European Court of Human Rights still requires nation-states to cooperate with it if it is to be effective.

- In 2011, the House of Commons voted by a majority of 212 *not* to comply with a judgment by the European Court of Human Rights that denying prisoners the vote was illegal. As an independent nation-state the UK was able to do this.

- The European Court of Human Rights has ruled that the UK's government's Investigatory Powers Act (2016) is illegal. However, Parliament, as the supreme law-making body in the nation, ignored the ruling.
- In 2015 Russia passed a law which states that its national law takes precedence over the judgments of the European Court of Human Rights.

Typical mistake

Do not confuse the European Convention on Human Rights and the European Court of Human Rights with the European Union. They are entirely separate.

The successes and failures of international tribunals

REVISED

Table 5.4 looks at international tribunals.

Table 5.4 International tribunals: successes and failures

Tribunal	Successes	Failures
Former Yugoslavia: this tribunal was established in 1993 to prosecute human rights abuses committed during the wars following the break-up of Yugoslavia.	By the time it closed in 2017, the tribunal had indicted 161 individuals and convicted 90 of them of human rights abuses. These included leading individuals such as the Bosnian Serb leader Radovan Karadzic (40 years) and the Bosnian Serb military commander Ratko Mladic (life).	The tribunal has been criticised by Serbia and Russia for being biased against Serbs and Bosnian Serbs. It has failed to encourage reconciliation in the Balkans. Critics claim that it represents victors' justice since potential war crimes such as the NATO bombing of Radio Serbia in 1999 have not been investigated by the tribunal.
Rwanda: from 1994 to 2015 this tribunal prosecuted the Hutus responsible for the genocide of approximately 800,000 Tutsis in Rwanda in 1994.	The tribunal convicted 61 people for the genocide. The tribunal also established a number of important legal precedents which will be important in the future development of international human rights law. Jean-Paul Akayesu became the first person to be convicted for the crime of genocide. The Rwandan prime minister, Jean Kambanda, was sentenced to life imprisonment. This developed the important precedent that heads of government cannot claim state immunity from prosecution. The tribunal also established that rape can be used as a way of perpetuating genocide and that the media can be prosecuted for encouraging genocide.	The tribunal has been criticised for only prosecuting Hutus. Allegations that when the Tutsi Rwandan Patriotic Front regained power it carried out mass atrocities were not investigated by the tribunal. Some critics have alleged that the Rwandan tribunal also represents victors' justice.
Cambodia: the Cambodian tribunal was set up in 2006. Although it is a national court it works closely with the United Nations. It prosecutes crimes against humanity, war crimes and genocide committed during the rule of the Khmer Rouge (1975–1979).	The tribunal has secured three convictions of leading figures in the Khmer Rouge government: ● Nuon Chea (chief ideologist): life sentence for genocide ● Khieu Samphan (former head of state): life sentence for genocide ● Kang Kew Lew (head of internal security): life sentence for crimes against humanity.	The tribunal has been criticised for only securing three convictions, at a cost of £232 million. Critics claim that there has been political interference in the work of the tribunal. The Cambodian prime minister since 1985 has been Hun Sen. He served as a military commander in the Khmer Rouge and has been accused of limiting the scope of the tribunal's investigations.

➜

Tribunal	Successes	Failures
Sierra Leone: this tribunal was set up in 2002 to prosecute human rights abuses which took place during the civil war in Sierra Leone.	The tribunal has sentenced the former president of Liberia, Charles Taylor, to 50 years' imprisonment for aiding atrocities carried out by the Revolutionary United Front in Sierra Leone. Taylor is the first head of state since Nuremberg to be convicted of crimes against humanity and war crimes. The tribunal also established important new principles in international law. It secured the first conviction for the use of child soldiers being a crime against humanity. It also defined forced marriage as a crime against humanity.	Most of the funding for the tribunal was provided by the United Kingdom and the United States. Charles Taylor's trial was transferred to The Hague and he has been imprisoned in the UK. Critics therefore claim that the tribunal has been too influenced by Western interests and that it has created a negative view of African justice.

Now test yourself

TESTED

5 What have been the most important convictions of the UN tribunal for the former Yugoslavia?
6 Why has the conviction of Charles Taylor been important in the development of international human rights law?
7 In what ways did the Rwanda and Sierra Leone tribunals develop important new principles in international human rights law?
8 What is 'victors' justice' and why have some tribunals been accused of this?

Answers on p. 108

Exam tip

If there is a section C question asking you to 'evaluate' the effectiveness of international courts and tribunals, you would gain A03 (evaluation) marks if you were able to explain *which* courts and tribunals have been most successful and *why*.

Cultural relativism

REVISED

- Cultural relativists claim that it is impossible to enforce an international standard of human rights because human rights are not universal. Instead nation-states determine the human rights of their citizens based on different cultural and religious traditions.
- The focus of the Universal Declaration of Human Rights, for example, is based on **European Enlightenment** traditions which emphasise the rights of the individual.
- This conflicts with Asian values, expressed in the Bangkok Declaration (1993), which emphasise the wellbeing of the community over the rights of the individual.
- The influence of the highly socially conservative Orthodox Church has also made Russia less tolerant of non-traditional gender and sexual choices than western European countries. African nation-states are similarly culturally conservative.
- World religions such as Islam and Christianity base human rights in religious teaching. Certain Islamic republics, such as Afghanistan, Iran and Pakistan, are ruled by Islamic law. The legal system of Saudi Arabia is based on Sharia law which is often in conflict with the Universal Declaration of Human Rights.

The **European Enlightenment** was an intellectual movement which took place in the eighteenth century and prioritised individual liberty and religious toleration. These principles have significantly influenced the development of international human rights-based law.

The rise of humanitarian intervention

REVISED

- Following the end of the Cold War (1989–1991) a number of **humanitarian interventions** took place. These suggested a more liberal world order in which the international community would be more united and be less likely to tolerate human rights abuses.
- Humanitarian intervention is founded on the moral obligation to 'save strangers'. It is based on a liberal belief in the importance of our shared humanity.
- In 1999, Tony Blair in his Chicago speech stated that 'acts of genocide can never be a purely internal matter'.
- In 2005, the UN World Summit published UN Responsibility to Protect. This states that 'each individual State has the responsibility to protect its populations from genocide, war crimes, ethnic cleansing and crimes against humanity'.
- This established the principle that the sovereignty of nation-states is 'conditional' upon them not abusing the human rights of their citizens. If this does occur, then the international community has the responsibility to intervene on behalf of the victims.
- UN Responsibility to Protect is important because it provides a legal justification for humanitarian intervention within a nation-state.

A **humanitarian intervention** is an intervention within the borders of a nation-state which is designed to achieve humanitarian rather than geostrategic objectives.

Why are some humanitarian interventions more successful than others?

REVISED

- In order to be successful, humanitarian interventions should be launched only when they have a good likelihood of success.
- It is therefore important that they are not motivated purely by liberal good intentions. This has sometimes been referred to as the 'CNN factor' and the demand that 'something must be done' to avert a humanitarian catastrophe. Instead a number of rational and pragmatic questions need to be asked before a humanitarian intervention is embarked upon.

Legitimacy

- Is there international and regional support for the intervention? An intervention which is backed by the United Nations or NATO will be able to claim a significant level of legitimacy.
- The intervention in East Timor in 2000 was provided with strong legitimacy by the United Nations.
- French interventions in Côte d'Ivoire (2011), Central African Republic (2013–2016) and Mali (2013–2014) have been mandated by the United Nations in order to restore order and stability.
- In 2011, UN Resolution 1973 authorised NATO to protect civilians in Libya. However, NATO's active encouragement of the overthrow of Colonel Gaddafi subsequently challenged the legitimacy of the intervention.

Sufficient forces and a robust mandate

- Is the intervening force going to be large enough and equipped with a strong enough mandate to end the suffering?
- The NATO interventions in Bosnia (1995) and Kosovo (1999) were successful because they were carried out with substantial military force.

- African Union and United Nations forces have been much less successful in Darfur (2007–) because they do not possess sufficient authority to actively intervene on behalf of the population.

Realistic objectives

- Are the objectives of the humanitarian intervention realistic and achievable?
- When British troops intervened in Sierra Leone in 2000 they were confronting criminal gangs and were supported by the government of Sierra Leone. Sierra Leone is also relatively small and is easily accessible from British bases and so it was clear that the intervention had a strong chance of success.
- Although substantial military forces were committed to Somalia in 1992, it was already a failed state and the massive and ungoverned size of the country made it impossible for US forces to enforce stability.
- The United Nations' biggest peacekeeping operation is in the Democratic Republic of the Congo, involving 16,215 UN troops (2019). However, the immensity of the country, complicated tribal, ethnic and clan rivalries and the involvement of neighbouring powers have undermined its effectiveness.

Commitment to nation-building

- Is the occupying force prepared to make a commitment to subsequent nation-building?
- NATO interventions in Bosnia (1995) and Kosovo (1999) were successful because once peace had been secured, NATO troops worked closely with the United Nations in a nation-building role.
- Bosnia became a United Nations protectorate, enabling systematic and far-reaching nation-building to take place.
- NATO's intervention in Libya in 2011 led to the overthrow of the Gaddafi regime. However, there was no subsequent commitment to nation-building, which ensured that Libya quickly degenerated into anarchy and civil war.

Table 5.5 looks at examples of both successful and unsuccessful interventions.

Table 5.5 Examples of successful and unsuccessful interventions

Successes	Failures
Large-scale NATO intervention in Bosnia (1995) created a cease-fire which enabled all sides to agree to the Dayton peace plan. NATO's extensive bombing campaign against the Serbian government stopped it from carrying out ethnic cleansing against the Kosovo Albanians. (1999). In Bosnia and Kosovo there was then a significant NATO commitment to nation-building. The British intervention in Sierra Leone (2000) was led by elite forces who were targeting criminal gangs. It was welcomed by the population and proved vital in ending its civil war.	In 1992 the United States intervened in Somalia to 'end the starvation' (President George HW Bush). When 18 US troops were killed in the Battle of Mogadishu there was not the political commitment to remain in Somalia and President Clinton withdrew American forces. The UN intervention in Bosnia (1991–1995) was not mandated to take offensive military action and so was ineffective. The UN commitment in Rwanda was too small to deter the genocide in 1994. It also lacked a mandate to take appropriate action.

➜

Successes	Failures
The UN-mandated intervention in East Timor (1999–2000) provided the legal framework for its transition to independence and democracy. UN forces were able to disarm criminal gangs by engaging in an effective peacekeeping operation. In 2011, President Laurent Gbagbo of Côte d'Ivoire was ousted by the French special forces, operating within a UN mandate, after he used violence to ignore the result of the presidential election. French intervention in Mali (2013–2014) was targeted at ousting Islamist militants from the country. It was requested by the Malian government and backed by the United Nations and the African Union.	The NATO intervention in Libya in 2011 led to the toppling of President Gaddafi but it was too limited to create the conditions for subsequent nation-building. Although intervention in Afghanistan (2001–) has primarily been in order to protect Western powers from terrorism, it has had a humanitarian dimension. However, the inaccessibility of large parts of the country, tribal violence and limited military forces have made nation-building very hard to achieve. The Democratic Republic of the Congo is a quarter of the size of the United States and underdeveloped so even a large-scale military commitment is unlikely to ensure stability.

Alleged Western double standards/reasons for selective intervention

REVISED

Humanitarian intervention has been criticised for representing Western double standards and hypocrisy.

- NATO intervened in Bosnia (1995), Kosovo (1999) and Libya (2011) to protect human rights. However, NATO has not intervened to protect the human rights of people living in Darfur or the Democratic Republic of the Congo. Critics claim this is because these regions are less strategically important to the West.
- In 1994 the remoteness of Rwanda and its lack of geostrategic significance discouraged a Western response to the genocide.
- Critics claim that France's intervention in Mali and Central African Republic against Islamist militants was primarily for geostrategic considerations.
- Western powers have not intervened to stop alleged war crimes by Israel in the Gaza Strip, although they have launched air strikes on President Assad of Syria for his alleged use of chemical weapons.

However, there are other more practical reasons for selective intervention.

- The failure of the American intervention in Somalia (1992–1993) demonstrates that interventions in civil wars are unlikely to achieve their objectives. There are good practical grounds for not intervening.
- Some humanitarian interventions (such as within Syria) risk escalating the conflict and so, it has been suggested, are best avoided.
- It is impossible to resolve some humanitarian crises, such as alleged human rights abuses in Tibet, because they take place within powerful nation-states.
- Therefore, selective intervention is not necessarily an example of Western hypocrisy/double standards.
- According to Douglas Hurd, UK Foreign Secretary 1989–1995, 'We should do good where we can, but not pretend that we can do good everywhere.'

Debate

Is humanitarian intervention justified?

Yes	No
Liberals argue that our collective humanity means that there is a moral obligation to 'save strangers'.	Realists argue that respect for state sovereignty is vital in maintaining global stability.
UN Responsibility to Protect (2005) states that nation-states have an obligation not to abuse the human rights of people living within their borders.	Interventions within a nation-state could escalate into a wider conflict involving other powers. This has been a powerful argument against a Western humanitarian intervention in Syria.
If human rights are not protected, then regional and global stability may be threatened by escalating violence.	Humanitarian intervention can be used to justify national self-interest. Russia has argued that NATO interventions in Kosovo and Libya were launched in order to increase its regional influence.
Humanitarian intervention can deter further human rights abuses. This will therefore create the conditions for a more stable world order.	Western double standards suggests that humanitarian intervention is hypocritical.
The failure of some interventions does not mean that interventions should never take place.	Humanitarian intervention often fails to achieve its objectives and can encourage further instability (Iraq, Somalia, Afghanistan, Libya).
Allegations of Western double standards does not invalidate the success of humanitarian interventions in Kosovo, East Timor and Sierra Leone.	It is immoral to risk the lives of your citizens in conflicts that do not concern your nation-state.

Debate

Is humanitarian intervention an abandoned project?

Yes	No
NATO has played a leading role in humanitarian interventions. It is now returning to its original purpose of resisting Russian expansionism. This suggests that it is unlikely to be able to take a dominant role in humanitarian interventions in the future.	Although large-scale interventions may be less likely, the US bombing of Syria in 2017 and 2018 over the alleged use of chemical weapons demonstrates that the United States can still be prepared to provide global moral leadership.
The failure of Western interventions in Iraq, Afghanistan and Libya has significantly reduced enthusiasm for this sort of military commitment.	French interventions in Mali and the Central African Republic demonstrate the success of humanitarian interventions in stabilising nation-states and confronting terrorists and militants.
Successful humanitarian intervention depends upon the United States' commitment to the principle. This has been undermined by President Trump's 'America first' strategy.	The potential for failed states becoming havens for extremist groups provides a continuing strong case for humanitarian interventions as a way of encouraging global security and stability.
The growing assertiveness in global relations of Russia and China makes UN-backed humanitarian interventions less likely. This is because, as Westphalian states, they value state sovereignty.	Insufficient humanitarian intervention in Libya, following the overthrow of President Gaddafi in 2011, has led to Libya becoming a haven for terrorist groups and so a major threat to regional security.
Russia and China are also increasingly prepared to oppose humanitarian intervention since they see it as a way of Western powers seeking to advance their own liberal interests.	Lack of intervention in Libya and Syria has led to a migrant crisis which has destabilised the European Union.
The shift in the balance of power towards Westphalian states such as China and Russia will make humanitarian interventions more difficult to launch in the future.	This suggests that there is still a strong case for humanitarian intervention because the alternative of not acting may lead to worse consequences.

Now test yourself

TESTED

9 Which humanitarian interventions have been most successful and why?
10 Which humanitarian interventions have been least successful and why?
11 In what ways do liberals justify humanitarian interventions?
12 In what ways has humanitarian intervention been criticised?

Answers on pp. 108–9

Exam tip

If you can make occasional references to important concepts such as Westphalian principles this will provide your writing with greater maturity. For more on the significance of the peace of Westphalia see the exam tip on p. 16.

Exam practice

Section A

1 Examine the criticisms that have been made of both the International Court of Justice and the International Criminal Court. [12]
2 Examine why humanitarian intervention occurs in some cases but not in others. [12]

Section C

3 Evaluate the extent to which international courts and tribunals are ineffective in upholding international human rights law. [30]
4 Evaluate the extent to which globalisation has made it more or less difficult to enforce a global standard of human rights. [30]
5 Evaluate the extent to which the case for humanitarian interventionism is undermined by allegations of double standards. [30]
6 Evaluate the argument that humanitarian intervention represents an unjustifiable intervention in state sovereignty. [30]

Answers and quick quiz 5 online

ONLINE

Summary

You should now have an understanding of the following:

- the sources and development of international human rights law
- why national sovereignty makes it difficult to enforce international human rights law
- the failures and successes of all the courts and tribunals covered in this chapter
- the significance of specific cases in international law
- the meaning of cultural relativism and why it makes it difficult to achieve an international standard of human rights
- the arguments for and against humanitarian intervention
- how to compare and contrast examples of failed and successful humanitarian interventions
- the reasons for selective humanitarian interventions: does the accusation of double standards undermine the case for humanitarian intervention?

6 Global governance: environmental

The challenge of climate change

- In recent years, scientists have become increasingly convinced that human activity is having a major impact on how the climate is changing.
- The climate has always changed, but there is growing evidence to suggest that mass industrialisation is dangerously increasing carbon levels which are warming the planet. This is leading to a dramatic rise in the levels of the 'greenhouse' gases carbon dioxide (CO_2) and methane which, if unstopped, could lead to irreversible temperature increase.
- Rising global temperatures will increase the likelihood of drought, make some parts of the planet uninhabitable, threaten resource and food security, and encourage extreme weather events such as flooding and hurricanes.
- They will also lead to a rise in sea levels, which is already threatening the existence of islands in the Pacific such as the Maldives. The Alliance of Small Island States (AOSIS) is lobbying hard at UN climate change conferences for more action to reduce temperature increase because their national existence is being threatened by the impact of climate change.
- Progress has been made in recognising the extent of the problem and developing strategies to deal with it. However, further progress is hampered by nation-states' unwillingness to commit to carbon-reduction policies which might damage their economies.
- It has also been difficult to create a consensus on how the burden of carbon reduction can be fairly shared between the developing and the developed worlds.
- The lack of supranational institutions which can compel nation-states to act in a certain way means that the resolution of the problem depends upon nation-states agreeing to put the collective good before their immediate economic self-interest. This can be difficult to achieve.

The role and significance of the UNFCCC

REVISED

- The **United Nations Framework Convention on Climate Change** was drawn up in 1992 and presented at the Earth Summit at Rio de Janeiro in 1992.
- The UNFCCC states that nation-states must 'stabilise' carbon emissions so that they do not irreparably damage the environment.
- To achieve this the UNFCCC sets up annual Conferences of the Parties at which nation-states come together to negotiate ways of reducing human-driven climate change. The most notable have been at Kyoto (1997), Copenhagen (2009) and Paris (2015).
- At the Marrakesh Summit in 2018, the Marrakesh Partnership for Global Climate Action was established. This recognises the importance of non-state actors such as city governments, investors and businesses in reducing carbon emissions.
- The Secretariat of the UNFCCC provides detailed research on various strategies which can be deployed to reduce carbon emissions.

United Nations Framework Convention on Climate Change (UNFCCC) is an international environmental treaty which was adopted at the Rio de Janeiro Earth Summit in 1992. It recognises the importance of keeping global temperature rise to a minimum and established a framework for regular climate change conferences to take place.

- The UNFCCC also monitors the carbon-reduction strategies of nation-states and the extent to which they fulfil the Intended Nationally Determined Contributions agreed at the Paris Agreement (2015).
- 197 nation-states have signed the UNFCCC, so although it has no binding power, it has considerable international legitimacy.
- According to the UNFCCC, carbon emissions should be reduced according to 'differentiated responsibilities and respective capabilities'. This is controversial because it has hitherto placed most responsibility for cutting greenhouse gases on developed nation-states.
- The difficulty of ensuring a fair and impartial reduction in carbon emissions which does not unjustly impact on the economic development of nation-states is a major challenge for the UNFCCC.

The role and significance of the IPCC

REVISED

- The **Intergovernmental Panel on Climate Change** was established in 1988. It is important because it provides detailed, scientific and impartial research on the way in which the climate is changing and what the impact of this is now and likely to be in the future.
- In 2018, the IPCC issued a stark warning that on current projections, temperature rise in the twenty-first century is likely to be closer to 3 degrees than the 1.5 degrees nation-states agreed to work on together at the Paris Agreement in 2015. According to the IPCC, this would lead to 'rapid, far-reaching and unprecedented changes in all aspects of society' and a 'climate catastrophe'.
- The 2018 report 'Summary for Policy Makers' is especially notable because it states that action must be taken *immediately* to stop irreversible harm to the environment. It also establishes what needs to be done to keep temperature rise at or below 1.5 degrees.
- This would mean investing 2.5% of global GDP to transform society and economy so that global emissions of CO_2 decline by 45% from 2010 levels by 2030. By 2050 there should be global net zero emissions of carbon.
- Since the scientists on the IPCC are nominated by nation-states in both the developed and the developing worlds, their reports represent balanced scientific opinion unconnected with the needs and priorities of particular nation-states. This gives their findings strong scientific legitimacy.

The **Intergovernmental Panel on Climate Change** (IPCC) was established by the United Nations in 1988. It provides impartial data on climate change and strategies to deal with it. Since it comprises expert scientists from across the world, it is a globally accepted authority on climate change.

Competing views about how to tackle environmental issues

REVISED

- Although there is agreement among environmentalists that the issue of climate change needs to be addressed, there are significant differences between deep and shallow green responses (see Table 6.1).
- **Deep green ecology** provides a radical approach to the environment based upon the philosophical principle that human beings are part of the ecosystem and so have a duty not to harm that which sustains them and all life.
- In contrast, **shallow green ecology** is reformist and is based on the practical proposition that the consequences of climate change will be

Deep green ecology is based on the principle that all life on Earth is of essential value. Human beings have a duty not to exploit the planet since they are part of the ecosystem, like all other living beings. Radical steps must be taken to limit humanity's impact on the environment in order to promote the sanctity of all life on Earth.

Shallow green ecology states that the environment needs to be protected in order to ensure that human beings prosper and survive. It is pragmatic rather than idealistic and is based on a human-centred (anthropocentric) approach to environmental issues. Its approach is much more self-centred than that of deep green ecology.

harmful for human beings and so the problem needs to be addressed. It is therefore more practical and less idealistic than deep green ecology.

Typical mistake

Students can make the mistake of suggesting that the main difference between shallow and deep ecology is simply that deep ecology wants to take more urgent action to protect the environment. There is some truth in this, but the main point of difference is that deep ecologists believe all life on the planet must be nurtured and protected as a moral imperative. Shallow ecologists support environmentalism simply as a way of protecting the wellbeing and survival of humanity.

Exam tip

Ecologism is one of the non-core political ideologies in Unit Two. Even if it is not the ideology that you are studying you could usefully familiarise yourself with the ideas of the deep and shallow ecologist thinkers. This will give your work on contrasting approaches to the environment greater conviction.

Table 6.1 Shallow green and deep green ecology compared

Shallow green (reformist)	Deep green (radical)
Shallow green ecology accepts that the actions of human beings are responsible for an increase in carbon emissions. Shallow green ecologists accept that development needs to be sustainable so that the existence and prosperity of future generations is not threatened by the actions we take now. Shallow ecology is based on the *practical* belief that the increase in global temperature has to be kept to a minimum in order to protect human beings as a species. According to shallow green ecology, governments and human beings can resolve the problem within existing free-market/capitalist structures. Shallow green ecologists take seriously the reports of the IPCC and believe that global action must be taken to confront the problem of climate change. This can be done by governments committing to renewable energy rather than fossil fuels, encouraging the use of electric cars, charging for plastic bags and introducing congestion charges in big cities. Individuals can also help reduce carbon emissions by eating less meat and fewer dairy products, flying less and choosing to use public transport. Shallow ecology sees climate change as a practical issue that can be successfully addressed without fundamental changes to how people live their lives. It is anthropocentric because it is centred on ensuring that climate change does not negatively impact on human beings. It makes no commitment to the wider biosphere.	In contrast to shallow green ecology, deep green ecology is founded upon the belief that, as part of the biosphere, human beings are responsible for protecting it. Human beings ought to do this not in order to protect themselves from the harmful impact of climate change but out of duty and reverence for the planet. We ought not to harm that which sustains us. Deep green ecology is not anthropocentric because it focuses on the importance of protecting the planet as an entity in itself. It does not draw a distinction between human beings and other forms of life. Therefore, it is ecocentric rather than anthropocentric and provides an idealistic approach to the environment. Deep green ecology is closely associated with the Gaia thesis of James Lovelock (1919–), which sees Earth as a living being, 'Gaia', which we must safeguard. Deep green ecologists demand a paradigm change in how human beings relate to the planet. Capitalism has exploited the planet and so needs to be fundamentally reformed. We ought no longer to use the planet for our own material advantage. Instead, we must become eco-literate so that we learn to put the good of the planet first. Deep ecologists see existing attempts to reduce carbon emissions as fundamentally flawed. This is because they are based on a human-centred desire to survive rather than genuine engagement with the needs of the whole biosphere.

The meaning and significance of sustainable development

REVISED

- **Sustainable development** is the principle that development today must not be allowed to irreparably damage the environment for future generations.
- The concept derives from the report of the Brundtland Commission, 'Our Common Future' (1987), and is at the heart of the work of the IPCC and the UNFCCC.
- The importance of sustainability was further recognised in 2015 when the Millennium Development Goals (2000–2015) were replaced by the Sustainable Development Goals (2015–2030).
- Sustainable development means that development cannot be measured in economic terms only. Instead, it must take account of the likely impact of what governments and individuals do today on the future of the planet.
- It is difficult to achieve sustainability because the consequences of how we act now will only be felt in the future. As a result, governments and individuals can often choose to concentrate on their own immediate wellbeing and so ignore the potential long-term impact on the **global commons**.

Sustainable development is a form of development which meets the needs of the present without sacrificing the wellbeing and survival of future generations.

Global commons refers to shared natural resources, such as the oceans and atmosphere, which are vital for the survival of the planet and yet are beyond the jurisdiction of any nation-state.

Intergovernmentalism is the process by which nation-states work together in collective institutions. Although they agree to cooperate, they retain their sovereignty and so cannot be compelled to act in certain ways. The more intergovernmental a regional organisation, the less it challenges state sovereignty.

Exam tip

Since the protection of the global commons is made difficult by the way in which nation-states prioritise their economic self-interest, it would be helpful to contextualise climate change within the realist/liberal debate. For liberals, climate change is a collective dilemma which requires nation-states to cooperate in order to resolve it. Realists are more sceptical of **intergovernmentalism** and are more likely to prioritise the immediate advantage of the individual nation-state.

Now test yourself

TESTED

1. What is the significance of the UNFCCC?
2. What is the significance of the IPCC?
3. Explain the tension between the shallow green (reformist) and deep green (radical) approaches to the environment.
4. What is sustainable development and why can it be difficult to achieve?

Answers on p. 109

The meaning and significance of the tragedy of the commons

REVISED

- The concept of the **tragedy of the commons** was developed in the 1830s by the economist William Forster Lloyd (1794–1852), who noted that the common land of England was being exhausted. This was because individuals were overgrazing the land in order to benefit themselves in the short term rather than considering the long-term impact on the good of the community.
- In 1968, ecologist Garrett Hardin (1915–2003) used the term 'tragedy of the commons' to explain how mankind's greed was depleting the resources of the global commons.

Tragedy of the commons is the principle that users deplete a shared resource system by acting out of self-interest instead of limiting what they take for the common good. The term is used to show how, by putting their own interests first, nation-states threaten the survival of the global commons.

- Since nation-states were putting their immediate interests above those of the collective good of humanity, the result would be the exhaustion of the planet.
- As a result, according to Hardin, 'freedom in a commons brings ruin to all'.
- The principle of the tragedy of the commons is very important in explaining why it is so difficult to achieve progress on climate change: nation-states and individuals prioritise their own immediate wellbeing and gratification.
- Because of this, they are often unprepared to take necessary action to limit consumption since they will face an immediate and measurable loss.
- There is also no certainty that if you do act, others will. Therefore, nation-states have often been unwilling to commit to drastically lowering their carbon emissions at climate change conferences because other nation-states may choose to do less.
- As a result, if nation-states do dramatically cut their carbon emissions, they may lose out in the immediate short term because other nation-states fail to act.
- The possibility that selfish states may choose to 'freeload' on the good intentions of other states makes it more difficult to encourage nation-states to take enough action to try to resolve the issue.
- Since the solution to the problem requires all nation-states to commit to limiting their carbon emissions, nation-states may rationally choose to carry on polluting since, without a global commitment, their reductions will make little difference anyway.

International climate change agreements

REVISED

Table 6.2 looks at the strengths and weaknesses of the various conferences on climate change.

Table 6.2 Climate conferences: a comparison

Conference	Strengths	Weaknesses
Rio de Janeiro (1992)	The Rio Conference (Earth Summit) recognised that climate change is a global problem. 172 nation-states attended the conference, including 108 heads of government. This provided the conference with global recognition and legitimacy. Participating governments were given the opportunity to adopt the UNFCCC. This committed signatory nation-states to attending regular climate change conferences in order to achieve progress on combatting climate change. Non-governmental organisations were also strongly represented, demonstrating their importance in developing strategies to protect the environment. The UNFCCC entered into force in 1994 and all members of the United Nations are party to it. This has been vital in ensuring that there are annual summits at which nation-states can try to achieve agreement on how to respond to climate change.	Although the Rio Summit recognised the importance of keeping global temperature rise as low as possible, it did not commit nation-states to legally enforceable target reductions. The summit also did not provide for a mechanism by which nation-states' strategies to reduce carbon emissions could be monitored. The way in which the Rio Summit put most of the responsibility on cutting carbon emissions on the developed world was highly controversial. This made developed nation-states, such as the United States, less willing to cooperate in future conferences since they felt that their economic growth was being unfairly restricted. The failure of the Rio Summit to achieve a consensus between developed and developing countries on how the burden of carbon reduction should be shared has been characteristic of all subsequent conferences.

→

Conference	Strengths	Weaknesses
Kyoto (1997)	The Kyoto Conference took the first practical steps in trying to resolve the challenge of climate change. It did this by providing 37 developed nation-states and the European Union with binding targets for carbon reduction. In the Kyoto Protocol, developed nation-states agreed that by 2012 they would cut carbon emissions by at least 5.2% on 1990 levels. The Kyoto Protocol made clear that resolving the issue of climate change was a global problem which would only be resolved through collective action. Kyoto was also important because it encouraged signatories to exceed their carbon targets. This was because of a scheme known as 'cap and trade' whereby nation-states that had failed to reach their targets would be able to purchase 'credits' from those that had beaten their targets. The financial incentive of 'cap and trade' also encouraged investment in green technology.	It was highly controversial that responsibility for combatting climate change was firmly placed on the developed world. The Kyoto Protocol's emphasis on the developed world meant that the emerging world, whose carbon emissions were significantly increasing as they industrialised, were exempt. Thus, China, India and Brazil were exempt from cutting their carbon emissions. During the treaty's lifetime China's carbon emissions increased by 300%. The different targets that the Kyoto Protocol required were also contentious. President George W Bush (2001–2009) regarded the ambitious 7% target that the United States was given as unfair and so withdrew from the Kyoto Protocol in 2001. For the Protocol to come into force it had to be agreed to by 55% of the world's carbon emitters. This was only reached in 2005 (eight years after the conference) when Russia signed.
Copenhagen (2009)	The Copenhagen Conference was important because it recognised that 'deep cuts in carbon emissions are required according to science'. Global temperature rise needed to be kept at 2 degrees above pre-industrial levels. The Copenhagen Accord also acknowledged that as emerging countries industrialised, so their carbon emissions were increasing. Therefore, they needed to be part of the solution. The developed and developing worlds would have to work together. This is why it was significant that the conference was attended by the leaders of the United States (President Obama) and China (Premier Wen Jiaboa). For the first time China and other emerging nation-states accepted that they also had a responsibility to cut carbon emissions. In total, nation-states responsible for 80% of the world's carbon emissions agreed to work towards cutting their emissions. In order to help the developing world adapt to green technology, the developed world would commit $100 billion in aid by 2020. A green climate fund was set up as part of this agreement.	Although the conference acknowledged that the issue of climate change needed to be addressed, it did not establish binding carbon-reduction targets. Nation-states which agreed to the Copenhagen Accord were required to submit their carbon-reduction targets by 2010. However, these targets were not binding and the Copenhagen Accord did not establish a mechanism for monitoring the extent to which targets were being met. There would also be no penalties for nation-states which failed to fulfil their commitments. Therefore, although the Copenhagen Accord's lack of enforcement mechanisms encouraged more nation-states to agree to it, its lack of coercive power also meant that nation-states were free to ignore their commitments. Although Copenhagen recognised the depth of the problem, it did not establish rigorous methods of enforcing carbon reduction. By respecting national sovereignty, the Copenhagen Conference failed to generate enough of a sense of urgency to resolve the problem of climate change.

➜

Conference	Strengths	Weaknesses
Paris (2015)	The Paris Conference recognised that temperature rise in the twenty-first century must be no more than 2 degrees and that nation-states should strive to ensure that it was no higher than 1.5 degrees. The conference accepted that carbon emissions must peak as soon as possible and that there must be a rapid reduction soon after. By 2019, 184 states and the European Union had ratified the treaty. Together they represent 88% of the world's carbon emissions. States that ratify the Paris Treaty decide what their carbon-reduction targets will be. These are known as Intended Nationally Determined Contributions and are supposed to be 'ambitious'. Nation-states' INDCs are then monitored in order to encourage compliance.	Nation-states are allowed to decide what cuts they are going to make rather than have them determined by a supranational authority. This has meant that nation-states have often not committed to extensive enough cuts in carbon emissions. As with all previous conferences, nation-states have been unprepared to agree to mandatory cuts in their carbon emissions to be enforced by an outside agency. In 2018, the IPCC announced that if the carbon-reduction commitments made at Paris were all fulfilled, global temperature increase in the twenty-first century would *still* be 3 degrees. Russia, which is responsible for 7.5% of global carbon emissions, has been criticised for very limited INDCs. In 2017, President Trump announced that the United States would withdraw from the agreement.

Now test yourself

TESTED

5 How does the tragedy of the commons help to explain why agreement between nation-states to limit carbon emissions is difficult to achieve?

6 Why do developed and developing countries find it difficult to agree carbon-reduction targets?

7 What is the significance of the Intended Nationally Determined Contributions agreed at the Paris Treaty (2015)?

8 Why did the Trump administration decide to withdraw from the Paris Treaty in 2017? Why is this significant?

Answers on p. 109

Obstacles to international cooperation

REVISED

Sovereignty

- An ongoing factor undermining attempts to cut carbon emissions is state sovereignty. Nation-states resent outside interference in their domestic policies. They have therefore been unwilling to accept supranationally imposed carbon-reduction targets and penalties for a failure to reach those goals.
- As a result, it has not been possible to establish binding and extensive carbon-reduction targets. The way in which nation-states put their sovereign self-interest before the good of the global commons is a key factor in making it difficult to resolve the problem of climate change.
- In 2017, President Trump announced that the United States was withdrawing from the Paris Treaty because of the damage which the INDCs were doing to the American economy.
- According to President Trump in 2017, continuing to observe the Paris Treaty would 'undermine our economy, hamstring our workers, weaken our sovereignty and put us at a permanent disadvantage to the other countries of the world'.
- In 2019, President Jair Bolsonaro of Brazil condemned President Macron's offer of international support to help Brazil put out its rainforest fires.

Responsibility

- The fact that the global commons reaches beyond national borders means that nation-states can abdicate responsibility for cutting carbon emissions. This is because they do not feel directly responsible for the global commons.
- Since the most damaging impact of climate change is likely to occur in the future, it is also difficult to persuade nation-states that they need to act quickly now. Although there is already some evidence of the negative impact of climate change, it is still incomplete and so nation-states often fail to treat the issue as urgent.

Developed versus developing worlds

- Developed and developing countries both need to reduce their carbon emissions in order to combat climate change. However, it has proved difficult to share the burden fairly between them.
- The developed world has been polluting the environment since the beginning of the Industrial Revolution in the eighteenth century. As a result, the developing world has argued that it is less responsible for climate change and therefore its carbon-reduction targets should be less.
- The priority of developing countries is economic growth and so they have focused more on lifting their citizens out of poverty than on reducing carbon emissions which could limit economic growth.
- The fact that coal is such a cheap source of energy in the developing world has led to a rise in its consumption in 2018 in important emerging economies such as India and China.
- Transnational corporations from the developed world opening factories in the developing world has made it difficult to determine responsibility for these emissions.
- The rapid growth of the developing world means that it is increasingly responsible for carbon emissions. However, because of the large populations, nation-states like India and China have been able to claim that their *per capita* carbon footprint is significantly less than that of the developed world.
- The key reason for President George W Bush's withdrawal from the Kyoto Protocol in 2001 and President Trump's withdrawal from the Paris Treaty in 2017 is that both believed that developing countries were not being expected to make the same level of commitment as the United States.

Role/significance of the global civil society and non-state actors in climate change

- A major success of the UNFCCC is that its annual summits have created unprecedented global appreciation of the scale and threat of climate change.
- Global pressure groups such as Greenpeace and Friends of the Earth lobby governments and ensure that the issue of climate change gains worldwide publicity. The Earth Day Movement was founded in 1970 and annually celebrates April 22 as Earth Day. The theme for 2019 Earth Day was 'Protect Our Species'.
- When British naturalist David Attenborough (1926–) presented 'Climate Change – The Facts' (2019), it demonstrated how trusted authority figures can be responsible for alerting the public and governments to the dangers of climate change.

- In 2019, *Time* magazine named Greta Thunberg among its list of the 100 most influential people on the planet for her work in alerting people to the more rapid than expected rise in global temperatures.
- The involvement of non-state actors in climate change conferences has meant that responsibility for reducing carbon emissions does not lie solely with nation-states. This is significant because nation-states have often been criticised for not taking enough action.
- In 2018, the United Nations announced that 7000 cities and 6000 companies had committed to cutting their carbon footprint. This suggests that reducing global carbon emissions is not simply an issue involving the decisions of nation-states.
- The C40 Cities Climate Leadership Group brings together 90 of the world's biggest cities to formulate strategies to reduce carbon emissions. In 2018, 19 of them announced that by 2030 all their new buildings would be carbon neutral.
- The Breakthrough Energy Coalition comprises a number of billionaire investors such as Bill Gates, Jeff Bezos and Richard Branson, and provides financial support to start-up companies that are developing the technology to reduce global carbon emissions by at least 500 million tonnes.
- The Clinton Foundation has established the Clinton Climate Initiative to develop public and private partnerships to cut carbon emissions, while also encouraging economic growth.
- The Global Apollo Programme was launched in 2015 by leading scientists such as Sir David King, the former chief scientific adviser to the British government. It calls upon developed countries to invest 0.02% of their GDP to fund projects to make electricity generation cheaper from renewable sources than from coal by 2025.

Debate

Is effective action being taken to resolve the challenge of climate change?

Yes	No
Climate change conferences have been successful in achieving a near global consensus that there need to be significant cuts in carbon emissions involving both the developed and the developing worlds. Since nation-states value their sovereignty and cutting carbon emissions could threaten their economic growth, this is a significant achievement. At the Paris Treaty the developed and the developing countries made significant commitments to reducing carbon emissions. The EU pledged to cut carbon emissions to 40% of 1990 levels by 2030. By 2050 it aims to be carbon neutral. India committed to cut carbon emissions to 40% of 2005 levels by 2030. China committed to cutting carbon emissions to 60–65% of 2005 levels by 2030.	Although the Copenhagen (2009) and Paris (2015) treaties acknowledged that global temperature increase has to be limited, mandatory targets on carbon limitation were not agreed. Instead, at Paris nation-states set their own INDCs. Although these are supposed to be ambitious, nation-states may decide on more cautious targets in order to protect economic growth. Russia's INDCs have been called 'critically insufficient' by the UNFCCC. In 2018, the IPCC announced that as a result of over-cautious INDCs, carbon emissions were likely to increase by 3 degrees in the twenty-first century. By 2030 the IPCC estimates the global temperature could already have risen by 1.5 degrees. President Trump announced in 2017 that the United States would abandon the INDC commitments it made at Paris at the earliest opportunity in order to boost economic growth:

➜

Yes	No
The climate change conferences set up by the UNFCCC and the reports of the IPCC have dramatically increased global awareness of the problem.	'We're not going to put our businesses out of work and we're not going to lose our jobs. We're going to grow; we're going to grow rapidly.'
The Extinction Rebellion (2019) and the global popularity and influence of Swedish teenager Greta Thunberg demonstrate growing public engagement in the issue. This indicates that governments are now more likely to be held accountable for any lack of action.	The failure of the United States to provide a moral lead on climate change has made it less likely that other countries will commit to ambitious carbon-reduction targets.
Attempts to limit carbon emissions are not confined to nation-states. The World Bank is focused on helping developing countries transition to low-carbon economies.	The relative cheapness of fossil fuels means that the developing world still often uses them to generate energy. In 2017 and 2018, China increased its consumption of coal to fuel its spectacular economic growth. This helped to make 2018 the worst year yet for global carbon emissions.
Non-state actors have also made significant progress on limiting carbon emissions.	Limiting carbon emissions will require people to accept significant lifestyle changes. This will be difficult to enforce because of the way in which globalisation has led to a rise in middle-class lifestyles in the developing world, so increasing global consumerism and materialism.
The C40 Cities Climate Leadership Group provides a forum for 90 of the world's biggest cities to work together to develop strategies to limit urban carbon emissions. In 2018, 27 of them announced that their carbon emissions had peaked and shown a significant decline in the previous five years.	Aircraft fuel is a major emitter of carbon and yet it is estimated that the number of people flying will increase from 4.3 billion in 2018 to 7.8 billion in 2036.
Global action groups also provide leadership on combatting climate change. For example, Breakthrough Energy Ventures is backed by investors such as Bill Gates and provides a $1-billion fund to encourage breakthroughs in green technology.	The increase of the global population from 7.3 billion (2019) to an estimated 9.7 billion (2050) will also lead to greater consumption of meat. The methane that cows produce already accounts for 5% of greenhouse gas emissions.
Requirements for green technology are necessitating the development of green capitalism. This is now providing consumers with enhanced opportunities to make green choices such as the purchase of electric cars and solar panels.	In 2018, the World Meteorological Organization announced that the years 2015–2018 were the warmest on record.

Exam practice

Section A

1 Examine the main differences between shallow and deep ecology. [12]

2 Examine the significance of the UNFCCC and the IPCC. [12]

Section C

3 Evaluate the extent to which climate change conferences have been effective in addressing the issue of climate change. [30]

4 Evaluate the extent to which disagreement between the developed and the developing worlds makes it impossible to resolve the issue of climate change. [30]

5 Evaluate the extent to which globalisation is making it more or less difficult to resolve the challenge of climate change. [30]

6 Evaluate the extent to which nation-states play the most prominent role in resolving the issue of climate change. [30]

Answers and quick quiz 6 online

ONLINE

Summary

You should now have an understanding of the following:

- the significance of the United Nations Framework Convention on Climate Change and the Intergovernmental Panel on Climate Change
- why it is difficult to achieve a consensus among developed and developing nation-states about limiting carbon emissions
- the distinction between the shallow green (reformist) and deep green (radical) approaches to the environment
- the meaning and significance of the tragedy of the commons
- the meaning and significance of sustainable development
- *in detail*, the significance of the most important climate change conferences (Rio de Janeiro, Kyoto, Copenhagen and Paris)
- the factors that held back further progress at these conferences
- the role of non-state actors in resolving the problem of climate change.

7 Power and developments

The meaning and significance of hard and soft power

- **Hard power** means the ability to achieve your objectives through coercion. This is done through the accumulation of military, economic and structural power since this can compel obedience.
- In the 1980s, the political theorist, Joseph Nye, contrasted hard power with what he called soft power. Soft power refers to the achievement of your aims through the attractiveness of your culture.

Hard power is the utilisation of military, economic and structural power to compel others to follow your will. It represents a coercive way of achieving power and influence.

Hard power

REVISED

- Realists have generally focused on the importance, in global relations, of hard power. This is because, according to realism, all nation-states are power-maximisers, and so the surest way of attaining your objectives is to forcefully compel the cooperation or obedience of other nation-states.

Military

- Military power provides an obvious example of how a nation-state can deploy hard power to achieve its purposes. In 2018, the United States spent more on defence than the total defence spending of the next seven countries combined. This demonstrates the importance that the Trump administration gives to military hard power.
- In order to stop President Assad from launching further alleged chemical attacks, President Trump bombed Syrian weapon sites in 2017 and 2018. The air strikes were also a strong signal to Russia and Iran that the United States was still a significant influence in the region.
- North Korean leader, Kim Jong-un, and President Trump threatening each other with nuclear weapons shows how the threat of military power can be used to bring about negotiations.
- In order to deter Russian expansionism, NATO has increased the number and scale of its military exercises. In 2018, Trident Juncture was the biggest exercise since the end of the Cold War.
- In 2018, the House of Commons Defence Select Committee recommended that UK defence spending should increase from 2% to 3% in order 'to keep this country safe'.

Economic

- Economic measures provide another example of hard power. United States aid programmes provide an important 'carrot' encouraging support for the United States in strategically important nation-states such as Egypt, Israel and Afghanistan.
- IMF/World Bank loans are conditional upon recipient nation-states adopting free-market structural adjustment programmes, demonstrating economic hard power influence.

- By investing in Africa, China is significantly increasing its strategic influence across the region. In 2018, at the China-Africa Forum for Cooperation, Beijing pledged $60 billion for African development aimed at further strengthening Sino-African relations.
- As the world's second biggest economy, representing 22% of the global economy (2018), the European Union wields enormous economic hard power. This gives it significant negotiating power on the World Trade Organization. It has also enabled it to negotiate the Transatlantic Trade and Investment Partnership on equal terms with the United States.
- Economic sanctions can also be used to coerce a nation-state. Extensive UN sanctions led to Iran negotiating a nuclear agreement in 2015. Since 90% of North Korea's exports go to China, Chinese sanctions have been significant in persuading North Korea to discuss denuclearisation.

The limits of hard power

- However, there are also limits to what hard power alone can achieve. The United States had overwhelming military superiority in Vietnam (1964–1975) and Iraq (2003–). However, it did not achieve its political objectives because it failed to win the support of the population.
- The defeat of Islamist terrorism will not be achieved solely through hard military power. The killing of terrorists can create so-called martyrs, which can encourage greater radicalisation. Extremism can therefore be conclusively defeated only if the extremist ideas behind it are successfully challenged.

Soft power

REVISED

- The coercive nature of hard power means that liberals have generally identified more with **soft power**. This is because soft power seeks to achieve influence more through persuasion and dialogue than through the maximisation of power.
- According to Joseph Nye, soft power is 'the ability to get what you want through attraction rather than coercion'. Instantaneous global communication means that soft power can have an immediate and powerful impact on global attitudes.
- The global appeal of American culture provides a good example of soft power. Hollywood, pop music and fashion have all contributed to the United States' global outreach because nation-states have often wanted to identify with the same values.
- In his 2009 inaugural speech, President Obama stated that American ideals of 'the rule of law and the rights of man. . . still light the world'.
- However, images on the internet of the horrific human rights violations carried out at the US prison at Abu Ghraib following the Iraq War (2003) show how the internet can suddenly and dramatically undermine a nation-state's soft power influence.
- Saudi Arabia has been criticised in the West for the murder of Jamal Khashoggi, human rights abuses and its poor record on female rights. In order to gain more favourable publicity, in 2019 Crown Prince Mohammed bin Salman appointed Saudi Arabia's first female ambassador to the United States, Princess Reema bint Bandar Al Saud.
- China has opened more than 500 Confucius Institutes across the world in order to spread an appreciation of Chinese language and culture.
- Royal weddings, tours and anniversaries are a major reason why the UK achieves so highly in terms of soft power.

Soft power is the ability to encourage others to support you by the attractiveness of your culture and the appeal of your political and economic institutions. It is persuasive, not coercive.

- The opening ceremony of the Olympics (London, 2012/Rio de Janeiro, 2016) provides a highly effective way for the host nation to expand its soft power influence. At the Winter Olympics in 2018, North Korea's cheerleaders presented a much more positive image of North Korea.
- Global television and the internet encourage the transmission of your values. The BBC is the world's most watched news channel, so contributing to Britain's global influence.

The limits of soft power

- In 2014, Russia's annexation of the Crimea was globally condemned and in 2018 it ranked only 28th in the world in terms of soft power. However, its nuclear capability, permanent membership of the UN Security Council and willingness to use military force can still enable it to achieve its strategic objectives.
- The Arab Risings (2011–) were initially influenced by Western liberal democratic values. However, President el-Sisi's use of the military to re-establish authoritarian rule in Egypt demonstrates the limits of soft power.
- In spite of Western condemnation of his regime, President Assad has been able to survive in Syria as a result of Russian and Iranian military support.
- Attempts by Western governments to encourage human rights in China have not been successful since they have not been backed up by hard power.

Smart power

REVISED

- In 2003, Joseph Nye coined the term 'smart power' to refer to the deployment of both hard and soft power strategies to achieve your objectives.
- According to smart power, the most effective way of gaining desired outcomes is to combine economic and military strength with positive diplomatic and cultural outreach.

Structural power

REVISED

- According to the political scientist Susan Strange, structural power refers to the way in which powerful nation-states can determine 'how things shall be done'. For example, global acceptance of the liberal economic principles of the Washington Consensus has enabled the United States to strongly influence the development of the global economy.
- This has also been facilitated by the United States having the biggest vote share on the World Bank and the International Monetary Fund.
- The United States' leadership role in NATO has further increased its global influence as the world's most influential military **superpower** (see Table 7.1).
- **Emerging powers** are now trying to acquire structural power in order to boost their influence. In 2015, China established the Asian Infrastructure Bank to enhance its economic and political impact on the developing world.
- The European Union also wields significant structural influence as the world's most advanced regional organisation. Other regional organisations such as ASEAN and the African Union have tried to emulate its liberal values.

A superpower maintains a pre-eminent position in global politics because it can project its influence anywhere in the world. Its influence cannot be rivalled by great powers and it has a strong sense of ideological self-belief.

An emerging power will have a fast-growing economy which provides it with the influence needed to aspire to great power status. An emerging power seeks to achieve enhanced global recognition of its growing influence on world affairs.

Table 7.1 Superpowers, great powers and emerging powers: the differences

Superpower	Great power	Emerging power
WTR Fox defined a superpower in 1944 as having 'great power and great mobility of power'. This means that a superpower can extend its influence anywhere in the world and at any time. A superpower will achieve this through the global deployment of considerable soft and hard power. A superpower will have strong structural power so that it can influence the 'global narrative' according to its 'world view'. Superpowers need a strong sense of ideological self-belief and the commitment to spread those values. Nation-states which aspire to be superpowers will also need to commit to taking the leading role in resolving global crises. A superpower's pre-eminent power sets it above other global powers and means that it can act independently of them.	Great powers will play the dominant role within their region and will have an influential role in global decision-making. They will be strongly represented on important institutions of global governance such as the United Nations, the World Trade Organization and the G7 and G20. They will have a forward foreign policy and a significant military influence. Their economic strength will also enable them to play an influential role in regional and global decision-making. Nevertheless, a great power will not be able to dominate other powers in the way that a superpower can. It therefore has less freedom of action than a superpower. A great power lacks the ability to act independently of other great powers.	An emerging power aspires to great power status. It will be self-confident and keen to play a more assertive role in regional and global decision-making. An emerging power requires high growth rates and an increasingly strong economy to enable it to support growing military and diplomatic outreach. Emerging powers will be increasingly consulted in international dialogue and will be strongly represented on intergovernmental organisations such as the G20. Most emerging powers are likely to be from the Global South since they will be challenging the dominance of international power by the Global North. This is why China could be said to be an emerging power as well as being a great power and potentially even a superpower.

Now test yourself

TESTED

1. What are the benefits and limitations of soft and hard power?
2. Why do you think India can be classed as an emerging power?
3. Why do you think the United States is a superpower and the United Kingdom is not?
4. What are the key differences between a superpower and a great power?

Answers on p. 109

Polarity: the implications for global order

REVISED

Unipolarity/Hegemony

- A unipolar distribution of power means that a superpower is so dominant in international relations that its influence cannot be challenged by any other power. In such circumstances a superpower is said to have achieved hegemonic status.
- The implications of **unipolarity**/hegemony for global stability divide political theorists. According to some, unipolarity can secure global stability because the hegemonic power can act as a global policeman and enforce obedience to international norms of behaviour.

Polarity refers to the way in which power is distributed in the system of international relations.

- A popular **hegemon** can also encourage 'band-waggoning' as other powers seek to emulate it. A hegemon can have a 'benign' impact on international relations.
- The unrivalled influence that the United States had at the end of the Cold War is generally seen as an example of the way in which a hegemon can encourage peace and stability. American values had a global appeal and the United States was able to provide uncontested global leadership in crises such as the first Gulf War (1991).
- However, critics suggest that unipolarity can undermine global stability because a hegemon has so much power that it can act in defiance of international law.
- The radical political scientist, Noam Chomsky, has advanced the theory that a hegemon can have a 'malign' or 'predatory' impact on international relations. In 2003, for example, the hegemonic power of the United States meant that it could invade Iraq in defiance of most world opinion.
- The implications of unipolarity can also depend upon the status and nature of the hegemon. A popular hegemon at the peak of its power will encourage global stability because there is no practical or ideological reason to contest it. This was true of Rome at the height of its influence when it maintained a 'pax Romana'.
- However, if a superpower is losing its hegemonic status, this can encourage other powers to challenge its influence. This creates a destabilising period of power transition as the hegemony may fight to maintain its global dominance.
- The Greek historian Thucydides argued that the Peloponnesian War was caused by power transition since 'what made war inevitable was the growth of Athenian power and the fear which this caused Sparta'.
- This is known as the Thucydides Trap because of the likelihood that a hegemonic power will fight to maintain its dominance from the growing ambitions of emerging powers.
- According to this principle, some historians have claimed that the outbreak of the First World War (1914–1918) was due to Germany provoking war by deciding to challenge a weakened United Kingdom for global hegemonic status.
- Today, the United States' loss of global economic influence may encourage emerging powers, such as China, to challenge its hegemonic status. This could have destabilising and dangerous consequences.

Unipolarity refers to a distribution of power in which one nation-state is so pre-eminent that it can assert its influence anywhere in the world and cannot be challenged by any other power.

A **hegemon** is a nation-state that has achieved such a dominant leadership role that it is able to extend its influence across the world and its supremacy cannot be realistically challenged by any other power. Since the end of the Cold War (1991), the United States has often been referred to as being the global hegemon.

Bipolarity

- A bipolar distribution of power means that two relatively evenly matched powers share power between them.
- Since, according to realism, all states are power-maximisers, realists favour **bipolarity**. This is because the expansionist instincts of two dominant rival states deter both of them from acting aggressively.
- Realists claim that the Cold War, between the United States and the Soviet Union (c1945–1991), demonstrates how bipolarity can maintain stability.
- Since they were so closely matched, neither side was prepared to risk war with the other. The tension between them created an equilibrium/balance of power which established powerful incentives for both sides not to risk war.
- India and Pakistan possessing roughly equivalent military power has, similarly, acted as a powerful deterrent to either side risking a full-scale regional confrontation.

Bipolarity occurs when two opposing superpowers contest global influence between them. Each superpower will seek to extend its influence at the expense of the other.

- However, liberals are critical of bipolarity because, they argue, peace is maintained only by the threat of massive retaliation. This creates suspicion and uncertainty, so undermining the effectiveness of intergovernmental organisations such as the United Nations.
- Events such as the Cuban Missile Crisis (1962) demonstrate how the tensions bipolarity encourages can lead to potentially cataclysmic consequences.
- Critics of bipolarity argue that it does not create the conditions for long-lasting stability since both sides are constantly preparing for war.

Multipolarity

- Liberals favour a multipolar distribution of power because they believe that nation-states are rational players and that they can cooperate in order to achieve mutually beneficial outcomes.
- A multipolar distribution of power means that no nation-state can act in defiance of international standards of behaviour. The fact that there is no one dominant force which can coerce others means that relatively evenly matched great powers need to work together to resolve collective dilemmas.
- Liberals also claim that a multipolar distribution of power increases the relevance and influence of intergovernmental organisations because nation-states will be more likely to use these to achieve mutually acceptable solutions. **Multipolarity** encourages multilateralism, which in turn encourages peace.
- However, realists regard multipolarity as the most dangerous distribution of global power. They see nation-states as being power-maximisers and so multipolarity encourages them to seek out the best possible alliances in order to increase their power.
- As a result, global relations are in a state of flux and uncertainty, making it more likely that nation-states will risk war since the balance of power is constantly changing.
- Since there are more 'players' involved, this further increases the likelihood of conflict between two or more of them.
- According to some historians, multipolarity may have caused the Second World War since Hitler believed that he could successfully challenge the existing distribution of global power.
- A number of powers (the United States, Russia, Iran and Turkey) have intervened in the Syrian civil war, further demonstrating how multipolarity provides few restraints on nation-states. This can encourage them to escalate military conflict in pursuit of their national interests.

Multipolarity means that a number of great powers share influence between them. No one power can claim hegemonic status and so the global distribution of power is evenly matched.

The changing balance of world order since 2000

REVISED

The United States

- There is a strong case to suggest that the United States can still claim hegemonic status because it can extend its influence anywhere in the world. It has more than 800 military bases in 70 countries and it has pre-eminent structural power in institutions of global governance such as the United Nations, the World Bank and the International Monetary Fund.
- It also has a strong sense of ideological self-belief and its global hard power influence means that it can provide a leadership role in

global dialogue and crisis resolution. The Trump administration, for example, has used its military outreach in the Pacific to put pressure on North Korea to negotiate over nuclear arms limitation.

- The cultural outreach of the United States ('Coca-Colonization') further provides it with unparalleled global scope.
- However, some critics have suggested that the United States is abandoning some of the requirements for hegemonic status.
- Since its interventions in Afghanistan (2001) and Iraq (2003), the United States has played less of a leadership role in global politics. Under President Obama, it did not intervene to support the pro-democracy movements in the Middle East during the Arab Risings (2011–). Lack of US intervention in Syria has enabled Russia and Iran to become the dominant forces in the region.
- President Trump's policy of 'America first' suggests a retreat from global leadership. His withdrawal from the Paris Climate Change Treaty (2015) and criticisms of NATO indicate a more isolationist approach to international politics.
- President Trump's imposition of tariffs on more than $250 billion of Chinese goods (2019) shows that the USA may now see economic globalisation as a challenge to American interests.

Exam tip

The policies of the Trump administration are interesting because they can be used to suggest that the United States is a declining superpower ('America first'). However, they can also be used to suggest that the United States is still an unrivalled hegemon (Trump's request to congress for a $750 billion military budget for 2020).

Emerging powers

REVISED

- It has been suggested that the global balance of power is being challenged by emerging powers. The economist, Jim O'Neill, has coined the terms BRIC (Brazil, Russia, India and China) and MINT (Mexico, Indonesia, Nigeria and Turkey) for these sorts of emerging powers.
- The growing economic power of the European Union may also be enabling it to become a major global influence.
- However, all of the emerging countries face unresolved problems which make it difficult for them to challenge for world influence.

China

- The Chinese economy is now the second biggest in the world after the United States. The way in which the Trump administration has provoked a trade war with China by putting extensive tariffs on Chinese goods demonstrates how threatened the United States feels by China's growth.
- China has established the Asian Infrastructure Bank (2015), which provides an alternative source of lending in the developing world to the International Monetary Fund.
- China is also challenging US influence in the South China Sea by militarising disputed reefs such as the Spratly Islands.
- After the United States, China is the world's second biggest spender on the military ($178 billion, 2020). China is also investing heavily in smart military technology such as cyber security in order to expand its global military influence.
- The China Belt and Road Initiative is designed to bring global trade dominance by creating a network of land and sea routes centred on China. Construction projects will take place in 71 countries and the total cost is estimated to be £760 billion. Such a grandiose project suggests that China is bidding for economic hegemony.
- However, Chinese military spending is still considerably less than that of the United States ($718 billion, 2020) and China has only

one military base abroad (Djibouti, East Africa) compared with 800 American ones.

- China has limited soft power outreach and its political system does not provide a 'beacon' cultural appeal that the United States has been able to claim.
- China is still a developing country and has significant domestic issues that it needs to resolve, such as a rapidly ageing population (as a result of its one child policy), environmental problems and widespread poverty.
- China is not yet the undisputed regional hegemon. Japan and South Korea have military alliances with the United States and Taiwan still asserts its independence from China. Before China could claim to be a superpower, it would need to be dominant in its near abroad.
- As a strongly Westphalian state which has generally opposed interventionism in the affairs of other nation-states, China is unsuited to the global leadership which is associated with superpower status.

Russia

- Under President Putin, Russia has reasserted its military and geostrategic influence. In 2015, Russia intervened in the Syrian civil war in support of President Assad. Russia has also established close ties with Iran as a counterweight to the United States in the Middle East.
- The Russian annexation of Crimea (2014) demonstrates Russia's growing military self-confidence. In 2018, Russia launched Vostok-2018, its biggest military exercise since 1981, involving 300,000 military personnel.
- However, although it has a strong nuclear arsenal, Russia's spending on defence is approximately 10% that of the United States. Russia has only ten overseas military bases and so lacks the global outreach and mobility of the United States.
- The Russian economy is highly reliant on the export of raw materials such as oil and gas. The strength of its economy is very dependent on the global price for these goods. This is generally seen as being a characteristic of a developing country and undermines Russia's potential for global influence. In 2019, Russia had only the 11th biggest economy in the world (behind Canada and Brazil).
- Unlike, the United States, Russia has limited structural power. Its lack of economic power means that it has a small proportion of voting rights on the World Bank and the IMF.
- Russia's strongly nationalist ideology lacks universal appeal beyond its near abroad.
- The Russian annexation of Crimea (2014), allegations that Russia has used cyber technology to destabilise foreign governments and allegations of state-sponsored criminal acts (including the poisoning of Sergei and Yulia Skripal in Salisbury in 2018) have significantly undermined the country's global influence.

The European Union

- The European Union economy represents 22% of the global total. This provides it with significant economic hard power. This can be seen in the way it negotiates as one body on the World Trade Organization.
- The European Union's strong record on democracy and human rights gives it strong cultural outreach (soft power).

- However, since EU foreign policy and defence are subject to the national veto, the EU has been unable to achieve a collective response to international crises and conflicts such as Syria.
- Most European Union member states prioritise their security through membership of NATO. This means that the EU lacks a shared military capable of asserting influence regionally or globally.
- The rise of populist/nationalist governments across the EU is also challenging the political coherence, further undermining its potential for global influence.
- The impact of Brexit on the future of the European Union is uncertain and makes it premature to suggest that the EU is likely to challenge the nature of world power.

Typical mistake

It is important to appreciate that superpower status is not simply about economic power and influence. A potential superpower will also want to provide global leadership rather than simply a dominant influence in its near abroad.

Debate

Has the rise of emerging powers decisively shifted the balance of global power?

Yes	No
The Russian annexation of Crimea (2014) and its military intervention in Syria (2015) on behalf of President Assad suggest that Russia is developing a more assertive foreign policy. Although the United States has been highly critical of the Assad regime in Syria, support from Russia and Iran has maintained it in power. China is expanding its military presence in its near abroad and is more assertively pressing its claims on Taiwan. The United States has failed to provide leadership in response to global crises such as the civil war in Syria, the Russian annexation of Crimea and the civil war in Yemen. The protectionist policies of the Trump administration indicate that the economic influence of the United States is being challenged by emerging economic powers such as China and the EU. China is challenging the United States as a major global investor. China built the African Union's parliament building in Addis Ababa. From 2005 to 2019, China lent South America $140 billion. This has increased China's global strategic influence. Emerging powers' military deployment of cyber technology is providing new opportunities to challenge the United States.	The military and strategic outreach of the United States is still unmatched. The United States is the leading nation-state in NATO, which is the world's most powerful military alliance. The United States also has unrivalled global alliances, including its military commitments in the Far East (Japan, Taiwan and South Korea), which limit China's influence even in its near abroad. The air strikes which the United States launched on Syria in 2017 and 2018 demonstrated that it has not abdicated influence in the Middle East to Russia. President Trump has taken the leading role in negotiating the denuclearisation of North Korea. The fact that the United States is able to deploy so much economic and military hard power against Iran indicates its continuing huge capacity for outreach. The US navy is the major presence in the Strait of Hormuz, through which almost 20% of the world's oil passes, so challenging Iran's regional influence. Emerging powers such as the European Union, India and Brazil have close links with the United States.

Now test yourself

TESTED

5 Why do realists favour a bipolar distribution of power over a multipolar distribution of power?
6 Why are the implications of unipolarity/hegemony for global peace and stability so contested?
7 In what ways can the United States still claim to be a global hegemon?
8 Which powers, and why, are most likely to be able to challenge the United States' hegemonic status. How realistic are these challenges?

Answers on pp. 109–10

The consequences for global order of the different systems of government

REVISED

Democratic states

- Liberal political theorists claim that **democratic states** are least likely to go to war with each other. This is because democratic states acquire their legitimacy from their citizens and, as rational human beings, we much prefer peace to war.
- This is known as the democratic peace thesis and suggests that the spread of democracies encourages the expansion of 'zones of peace' at the expense of 'zones of conflict'.
- Democracies are also more likely to fully commit to the success of institutions of global governance such as the United Nations.
- In 1992, Francis Fukuyama suggested in *The End of History and the Last Man* that the spread of liberal democracy would ensure that war and conflict would be consigned to history as states increasingly lived together in democratic harmony.
- Liberals also argue that autocratic/non-democratic states pose a greater threat to peace and stability because their 'legitimacy' derives from military triumph rather than democratic consent. This encourages them to risk war in order to justify their existence.
- China, it could be argued, is expanding its military influence in order to achieve the enthusiastic approval of its citizens. This will therefore make them more ready to accept their lack of democratic rights.
- Under President Putin, Russia's government has become significantly more authoritarian and, as a **semi-democratic state**, its foreign policy has become increasingly nationalist and assertive in order to encourage public support.
- However, realists claim that *all* nation-states are power-maximisers. Therefore, the type of government is irrelevant. India and Pakistan are both democracies and yet their rival claims over Kashmir provide an ongoing source of potential conflict between them.
- The eagerness of the United States to spread the principles of liberal democracy (Vietnam and Iraq) suggests that the expansion of democratic principles can also be destabilising.
- Autocratic governments have most to lose from risky military gambles. In 1982, the Argentinian dictatorship was defeated by the British in the Falklands War. This led to its overthrow. In contrast, the Suez failure (1956) simply led to the replacement of Anthony Eden by Harold Macmillan.

A **democratic state** is one in which the government is elected by the public and is held accountable by them in regular, free and fair elections.

A **semi-democratic state** contains elements of a democratic and an authoritarian state. A non-democratic state provides no opportunities for its citizens to hold the government accountable for its actions.

Rogue states

- It is alleged that **rogue states** such as North Korea and Iran challenge world peace because they threaten their neighbours, do not accept international law and have illegally sought to acquire nuclear weapons in defiance of the Nuclear Non-Proliferation Treaty (1968).
- The term 'rogue' state is controversial, however. Critics claim that the United States has termed states like North Korea and Iran 'rogue' in order to undermine their legitimacy.
- However, other powers that have broken the Nuclear Non-Proliferation Treaty (India and Pakistan) have not been accused by the United States of being 'rogue'. This suggests that it is a subjective not an objective term.

A **rogue state** does not act according to international norms of behaviour and acts in defiance of international law. It will lack democratic legitimacy, have an aggressive foreign policy and links to terrorist organisations, and be seen as a threat to regional and global stability.

- According to some political commentators, the controversial invasion of Iraq by the United States (2003) and its unilateral withdrawal from the Iranian Nuclear Agreement in 2018 suggests that the United States also possesses some of the attributes of a rogue state.
- The way in which Iran and North Korea have been prepared to use their nuclear arsenals as a powerful bargaining tool suggests that their governments place them within a realist and rational tradition.

Failed states

- **Failed states** are those in which law and order no longer operates. They pose a considerable challenge to world peace because extremist/terrorist organisations can establish bases in them.
- The September 2001 al-Qaeda attacks on New York and Washington DC were plotted in Afghanistan after its central government collapsed. Failed states such as Somalia and Libya provide a haven for extremist groups to plan terrorist outrages.
- The way in which outside powers can intervene in failed states to advance their security interests can destabilise the balance of power. A number of great powers (Iran, Turkey and Russia) have intervened in the Syrian civil war, significantly increasing regional and global instability.
- The breakdown of government in Yemen has increased tensions in the Middle East as Saudi Arabia and its Sunni allies support the government against the Shia Houthi rebels. By doing this Saudi Arabia is seeking to limit the growth of Iranian influence in the region.

A **failed state** is one in which government has entirely broken down. Law and order cannot be maintained, public service cannot be provided and there is regular, uncontrollable violence.

Exam tip

This chapter's focus on the significance of power in global relations means that you will achieve most highly in the exam if you place your answers strongly within the context of liberal and realist debate.

Development and spread of liberal economics, the rule of law and democracy

REVISED

- At the end of the Cold War, President George HW Bush (1989–1993) referred to a 'New World Order'. This would be based on American values such as economic liberalism (the Washington Consensus), democracy, human rights and the rule of law.
- These were driven forward by the expansion of the World Trade Organization, humanitarian interventions, enhanced regionalism and the spread of democracies.
- However, the global financial crisis (2007–2008) and the growing self-confidence of China and Russia have challenged Fukuyama's thesis that the triumph of free trade and democracy is inevitable.

In what ways do developments in global power impact on contemporary issues?

- Since 2000, US hegemony has been challenged by emerging powers. Liberals have generally seen the creation of a more multipolar world as an effective way of resolving issues involving conflict, poverty, human rights and the environment.
- This is because there is no bipolar tension between powers and so they can come together in institutions of global governance to resolve collective dilemmas.
- The Paris Treaty (2015) provides a good example of great powers working together to address the issue of climate change.
- However, realists are more negative about the way in which the balance of global power is changing. Emerging powers are becoming

more confident about advancing their own interests, as the United States becomes increasingly unwilling to fulfil the role of world policeman. Periods of power transition can thus undermine liberal attempts to collectively resolve problems.

- The Trump administration has put what it sees to be its own national interests first by withdrawing from the Paris Treaty (2015) and abandoning the principles of free trade. The Trump administration has also condemned the liberal/universalist principles on which the United Nations is established.
- As a result, there is a lack of global leadership and nation-states advance their own strategic interests and cultural values. This makes it much more difficult to resolve collective dilemmas.
- For example, the intervention of Russia and Iran in Syria demonstrates how both powers are seeking to advance their national interests in the Middle East. Saudi Arabia's air strikes in Yemen against the Houthi opposition rebels is designed to stop Iran gaining influence in Yemen.
- Turkey's military offensive against the United States' Kurdish allies in Syria in 2019 demonstrates declining respect for American global influence and interest.
- China is challenging US influence in the South China Sea in order to be recognised as the main power in that region.
- Emerging powers trying to increase their regional influence creates instability and tension. This is because it may provoke conflict as the United States seeks to protect its hegemonic status. The trade war that broke out between the United States and China in 2018 is an example of this.

Now test yourself

TESTED

9 Why do liberals believe that democracies provide the best way of preserving global peace and stability? Do you agree?
10 Why is the term 'rogue state' controversial?
11 Why do failed states threaten peace and stability?
12 What evidence suggests that world politics are in a period of power transition? Why do realists believe that this poses threats to peace?

Answers on p. 110

Exam practice

Section A

1 Examine the main differences between soft and hard power. [12]
2 Examine the differences and similarities between great powers and emerging powers. [12]

Section C

3 Evaluate the extent to which a unipolar distribution of power is more likely to secure peace and security than a bipolar distribution of power. [30]
4 Evaluate the extent to which the United States is still able to claim global hegemonic power. [30]
5 Evaluate the extent to which emerging powers have significantly changed the global balance of power. [30]
6 Evaluate the extent to which failed and rogue states pose the greatest challenge to global stability. [30]

Answers and quick quiz 7 online

ONLINE

Summary

You should now have an understanding of the following:

- the distinction between soft, hard, smart and structural power
- the differences between a superpower, a great power and an emerging power, with examples of all three
- the differences between a unipolar, bipolar and multipolar distribution of global power and the way in which they can impact on international peace and security
- the extent to which the United States can still claim global hegemonic power
- the extent to which China can now claim superpower status
- the extent to which emerging powers have significantly altered the distribution of global power
- the different categorisations of nation-states (democratic, semi-democratic, non-democratic, autocratic, failed and rogue)
- whether the above characteristics of nation-states are significant in terms of maintaining global peace and security.

8 Regionalism and the European Union

The growth of regionalism and its different forms

- **Regionalism** is the process by which nation-states inhabiting the same geographical area decide to work together in regional organisations in order to achieve collective positive outcomes.
- As members of regional organisations, nation-states agree to put certain limits on their **sovereignty**. In advanced examples of regionalism, such as the European Union, the limits placed on national sovereignty can be extensive. In less ambitious regional organisations, such as the Arab League, these limitations are much less significant.
- There are three main types of regionalism: economic, security and political.
- However, there can be a considerable overlap between them. The EU and ASEAN, for example, combine all three characteristics.

Regionalism is the process by which nation-states in the same geographical location agree to establish shared governing institutions which will create greater cooperation and understanding between them.

Sovereignty refers to total power and authority. According to the principles of the Peace of Westphalia (1648), nation-states have traditionally been sovereign over everything that occurs within their borders.

Economic regionalism

REVISED

- Economic regionalism is the process by which nation-states eliminate trade barriers (tariffs) between them in order to encourage greater regional trade. This will increase investment and contribute to stronger regional economic growth.
- Liberals claim that economic regionalism is also an important way of encouraging cooperation, stability and peace — when nation-states trade freely, they are less likely to go to war with each other.
- According to the classical liberal economist Frédéric Bastiat (1801–1850), 'If goods do not cross borders, armies will.'

Security regionalism

REVISED

- Security regionalism can enhance the security of a region by encouraging security cooperation within a region.
- A good example of this is the Organization for Security and Co-operation in Europe (OSCE), which brings together the United States and Canada with European and central Asian nation-states. It provides a forum in which its 57 member states (2019) can try to resolve crises which might threaten peace within the region.
- Security regionalism can also mean the establishment of a security alliance against external aggression.
- NATO is an example of this because it commits its membership to 'collective security' against outside military challenges.

Political regionalism

REVISED

- Political regionalism enables distinct parts of the world with shared political and cultural values to represent them more forcefully in global relations.

- The Arab League and the African Union both provide a way in which Arab and African opinion can be represented in international dialogue.

The significance of regionalism

REVISED

The relationship between regionalism and globalisation

- The challenges and opportunities created by globalisation have encouraged the spread and development of regional organisations.
- Regionalism can enable member states to take better advantage of economic globalisation. The European Union, for example, represents the interests of all its members on the World Trade Organization, which gives it more power to negotiate favourable trade deals.
- The European Union has been negotiating the Transatlantic Trade and Investment Partnership with the United States as one body. This has given the European Union considerably more economic leverage than if its member states made independent trade agreements with the United States.
- Economic regionalism can also protect a region from competition from other parts of the world. The European Union has a common external tariff and the Common Agricultural Policy subsidises European agriculture, so encouraging its consumers to buy European food.
- Regionalism can provide nation-states with a way of protecting their workers from being exploited by transnational corporations. The European Social Chapter, for example, means that workers' rights are equally protected across the whole of the European Union.
- Political regional organisations, such as the Arab League, encourage culturally and ethnically linked parts of the world to maintain their distinct heritage in response to cultural homogenisation and Americanisation.
- As globalisation makes borders more porous, it has left nation-states more vulnerable to drug trafficking, terrorism, organised crime and the spread of weapons of mass destruction.
- Regional organisations allow nation-states to coordinate their responses to these sorts of threats. ASEAN shares intelligence through its 'Our Eyes' programme. Europol coordinates intelligence gathering and crime prevention among the members of the European Union.
- Regional organisations can therefore provide ways in which nation-states can maximise their national interest through interdependence. This suggests that regional organisations can have a realist as well as a liberal purpose.

Development of regional organisations

REVISED

NAFTA/USMCA

- The North American Free Trade Agreement was established in 1994 to increase trade between the United States, Canada and Mexico by eliminating most tariffs between them. Its purpose was therefore purely economic and it was not designed to provide members with a greater shared political identity.
- NAFTA has been successful in sharply increasing the value of trade between its three members, from $290 billion in 1993 to $1.1 trillion in 2016. During the same period US foreign direct investment in Mexico increased from $15 billion to $100 billion.

- However, critics of NAFTA argue that it has led to significant job losses and wage stagnation in the United States as US manufacturers have been forced to compete with low-wage competition from Mexico.
- As early as the 1992 US presidential election, independent candidate Ross Perot warned American manufacturers that if 'you don't care about anything but making money, there will be a giant sucking sound going south'.
- President Trump agreed, calling NAFTA 'perhaps the worst trade deal ever made'.
- In 2018, pressure from President Trump led to NAFTA being renegotiated. It has been replaced by the United States, Mexico, Canada Agreement (USMCA).
- The way in which the United States, Canada and Mexico sought the best possible terms for themselves when negotiating USMCA suggests that they have only agreed to work together for their national advantage.
- NAFTA/USMCA is thus unlikely to develop a sense of regional identity between the United States, Canada and Mexico and so it is a very limited example of regionalism.

African Union

- In 1963, the Organisation of African Union (OAU) was established. Its main focus was ending colonial rule in Africa and encouraging closer cooperation between the newly independent states.
- In 2002 it was replaced by the African Union, which is more economically and politically ambitious. The AU's Charter commits it to achieving 'greater unity, cohesion and solidarity between the African countries and African nations'.
- The structures of the AU are closely modelled on those of the EU. The AU's main decision-making body is the Assembly of the African Union, which all African heads of government attend. Its Pan-African Parliament debates issues and provides advice to the Assembly. The AU's Commission implements AU policies and decisions.
- The AU's Peace and Security Council provides a mechanism for African Union forces to intervene in member states to stop genocide and crimes against humanity being committed.
- The AU's New Partnership for Africa's Development (NEPAD) encourages greater regional trade and integration between member states.
- The AU has ambitious plans to establish a single market, to be followed by a full customs union and then monetary union, which would be administered by an African central bank.
- However, there are major obstacles to the further development of the African Union.
- In 2019 there were 54 African nations covering a continent and at very different stages of development. European integration began with just six members of the European Economic Community (EEC), all of which were already at an advanced stage of development.
- Tribal and ethnic differences which have provoked genocide in Rwanda, civil war in the Democratic Republic of the Congo and crimes against humanity in Darfur suggest that the AU lacks a common sense of identity necessary for enhanced cooperation.
- African rulers have been criticised for their lack of commitment to democracy and for extensive corruption. It is unlikely that they will

embrace African unity as this would significantly reduce their power and influence.

- In 2004 the AU's African Court of Justice and Human Rights was established. However, the fact that the AU has tolerated significant human rights abuses in Zimbabwe under President Mugabe, Libya under President Gaddafi and Sudan under President Omar al-Bashir suggests that the AU puts the interests of dictators before pan-African unity.
- The Treaty of Rome (1957), which established the EEC, made a commitment to 'ever closer union'. In contrast, the charter of the African Union (2002) is committed to defending 'the sovereignty, territorial integrity and independence of its member states'.

Arab League

- The Arab League was set up in 1945. It has 22 members (2019) and is an example of security and political regionalism because its main focus is on resolving disputes within the Arab world and representing the interests of Arab states on the world stage.
- The Council of the Arab League, which is made up of representatives of each state, meets twice every year. The Arab League also has a permanent secretariat headed by a secretary-general.
- In 2011 the Arab League agreed to suspend Syria from membership because of President Assad's killing of protestors.
- In 2011 Libya was also suspended from membership as a result of President Gaddafi's attacks on the civilian population. The Arab League then supported the UN's imposition of a no-fly zone on Libya.
- The Arab League has supported Saudi Arabia's military intervention in Yemen against the Houthi rebels.
- In 2019, the first ever summit between leaders of the European Union and the Arab League took place in Egypt. The focus of the conference was on establishing a shared response to security, migration and environmental challenges.
- However, the political influence of the Arab League is very limited. Decisions taken on the Council are binding only on those members which supported them. When it does agree resolutions, they rarely commit its members to action.
- The Arab League has also failed in its key role in encouraging peace in the Middle East. It could not achieve a consensus on how to respond to the 1991 and 2003 Gulf Wars.
- Attempts by the Arab League to mediate a ceasefire in the Syrian civil war also achieved nothing. Instead Iran and Russia became the main players in the conflict, further marginalising the influence of the Arab League.
- The Arab League has failed to intervene effectively to restore stability within post-Gaddafi Libya. It has also failed to take coordinated military action against Islamic State.
- The Arab League's recognition of Palestine as a state has meant it has had no political leverage with Israel in trying to drive forward a peace process.

ASEAN

- The Association of Southeast Asian Nations dates from 1967. It has increased from five to ten members (2019).
- ASEAN was established to boost prosperity and encourage 'friendship and cooperation' among its members. Its leaders meet twice a year at an ASEAN summit.

- ASEAN's Regional Forum enables member states to work with other regional powers, such as China and Japan, to peacefully resolve regional disputes. All members of ASEAN are committed to nuclear non-proliferation and share counter-terrorism intelligence.
- Members of ASEAN have negotiated free-trade agreements between themselves and with neighbouring powers, including China.
- In 2018, ASEAN was collectively the sixth biggest economy in the world.
- However, ASEAN's commitment to an eventual free market is undermined by huge discrepancies in economic development between highly developed member states such as Singapore and much less developed states like Cambodia.
- Further integration is hampered by the different political systems of its members. For example, Vietnam and Laos are communist and Malaysia is a democracy.
- ASEAN's diplomatic regional influence is also weakened by significant differences between its member states. Cambodia has close ties with China, whereas the Philippines are closely aligned with the United States. This means that ASEAN has not been able to coordinate an agreed response to Chinese military expansion in the South China Sea.
- ASEAN is committed to the principle of non-interference in its members' domestic affairs and so has been criticised for not suspending Myanmar for its treatment of the Rohingya Muslims.
- Since the key decision-makers in ASEAN are its heads of government, it lacks the supranational institutions to further integrate in the way in which the European Union has.

Now test yourself

TESTED

1. Why was NAFTA established and why were its terms renegotiated in 2018?
2. What are the aims of the African Union and to what extent has it achieved them?
3. Is the Arab League a successful example of political and security regionalism?
4. Why was ASEAN established and to what extent has it developed since then?

Answers on p. 110

In what ways does regionalism challenge state sovereignty?

REVISED

- Regional organisations with strong supranational institutions reduce the sovereignty of member states.
- For example, the European Union is based on powerful supranational bodies such as the European Commission, the European Court of Justice and the European Central Bank. Member states have to accept the jurisdiction of these bodies over their domestic affairs.
- In the European Union, the 19 members of the Eurozone have to accept a common interest rate which is set by the European Central Bank in Strasbourg.
- Member states of the European Union have to accept the rulings of the European Court of Justice in areas where legal sovereignty has been pooled.
- Other regional organisations have also become more integrated, so challenging the sovereign independence of its members.

- Members of ASEAN have significantly reduced regional tariffs between them and increasingly work together on security issues.
- The African Union closely models itself on the European Union and plans to establish a single market and a single currency by 2023.
- The AU established a Peace and Security Council in 2004 and AU peacekeepers have served in Somalia, Burundi and Darfur.

In what ways does regionalism not challenge state sovereignty?

REVISED

- Most regional organisations do not have powerful supranational institutions like the **European Union**.
- The way in which they are organised is much more intergovernmental. This protects the sovereignty of the member states.
- In ASEAN, decisions are generally reached by its heads of government at summit meetings. This means that ASEAN lacks the governmental institutions necessary to challenge the sovereignty of its member states.
- In spite of the fact that the African Union has committed itself to a single market and a single currency, African leaders have been very unwilling to accept restraints on their sovereign independence.
- NAFTA was established to promote trade rather than share sovereignty. The United States, Canada and Mexico joined it with no higher purpose than to advance their own economic interests.
- Although the Arab League is committed to developing closer relations between its member states, its Charter also commits it to 'safeguard their independence and sovereignty'.
- Realists also suggest that nation-states join regional organisations in order to advance their national interests rather than because of a liberal commitment to sharing sovereignty.
- It has been claimed that Balkan states, such as Serbia and Montenegro, have applied to join the European Union because they see major advantages in being part of the European single market rather than from a shared commitment to 'ever closer union'.
- Security regional blocs, such as the Shanghai Cooperation Organisation (SCO) or NATO, are established to defend the national sovereignty of member states. They therefore protect rather than dilute national sovereignty.

The **European Union** is a political, economic and strategic regional organisation. Committed to 'ever closer union' it is the most developed regional organisation in the world.

Formation and development of the EEC/EU

REVISED

- The European Economic Community/European Union is the world's most liberal example of regionalism, its origins firmly rooted in a desire to challenge the nationalism which devastated Europe in the First and Second World Wars.
- In 1950 the Schuman Declaration established the European Coal and Steel Community (1951) which, by linking German and French industrial production, would make war between them impossible.
- According to the Schuman Declaration, the pooling of French and German coal and steel production would be the 'first concrete foundation of a European federation indispensable to the preservation of peace'.
- In 1957, the Treaty of Rome took the principles of the Schuman Declaration further. It created a free-trade area in goods between them and established the principle of a common external tariff.

- From its beginnings the EEC included **supranational** institutions such as the European Commission and the European Court of Justice to which member states would be accountable.
- As a result of the Treaty of Rome's commitment to 'ever closer union', the Maastricht Treaty (1992) significantly sped up the process of **European integration**. A common citizenship was introduced and, significantly, the Europe was renamed a Union rather than simply a Community.

Supranationalism refers to power being given to an authority which is above the nation-state and can compel its obedience. Regional institutions with advanced supranational institutions are most able to dilute state sovereignty.

European integration is the process by which 'ever closer union' is encouraged by the establishment of supranational bodies which legally, politically and economically create greater unity between the European nation-states.

Exam tip

The way in which Europe was devastated by two World Wars in the first half of the twentieth century gives the European regionalism a moral purpose which is lacking in other regional organisations. This might be seen as making European regionalism unique.

The functions of the EU's main institutions

The various institutions of the EU are outlined in Table 8.1.

Table 8.1 The EU's main institutions

The European Commission (supranational)	The European Commission is the executive (government) of the European Union. Each member state chooses a commissioner who represents a particular area, such as trade or transport. The Commission proposes legislation to the European Council of Ministers and the European Parliament and implements European law. Commissioners represent the interests of the EU rather than their national interests. The president of the Commission is nominated by the European Council and must then be approved by the European Parliament.
The European Council of Ministers (supranational/ intergovernmental)	The European Council of Ministers shares a legislative role with the European Parliament. It decides whether or not to adopt proposals made by the Commission and has to agree to the EU budget. Each member state sends the appropriate minister to meetings of the European Council of Ministers. For example, when the Council is discussing agricultural issues, Europe's ministers of agriculture will attend. Member states can represent their national interests here and some issues still require unanimity, so protecting national sovereignty. Increasingly, though, decisions on the Council of Ministers are being made by qualified majority voting.
The European Parliament (supranational)	The European Parliament is the only directly elected body in the European Union. Its influence has increased since it was created in 1979 and on most Commission proposals it now shares equal legislative power with the European Council of Ministers. It scrutinises the work of EU institutions and its consent is also required for the EU budget to be passed. The European Parliament approves and can dismiss the Commission.
The European Council (intergovernmental)	The European Council meets at least four times every year. It represents all of the EU heads of government and determines the strategic objectives of the EU. Since the Lisbon Treaty (2009), the European Council has elected its own president. Decisions taken on the Council need to be unanimous so this is the EU's main intergovernmental institution.
The European Court of Justice (supranational)	The European Court of Justice is the judicial arm of the European Union. Each member state sends a judge to Luxembourg where the court sits. It ensures that European law is equally enforced on all member states. In cases of dispute, the European Court of Justice can overrule domestic law since European law takes precedence.
The European Central Bank (supranational)	The European Central Bank is based in Frankfurt and controls the monetary policy of the 19 member states in the Eurozone (2019). It sets Eurozone interest rates and its central purpose is to maintain price stability.

Exam tip

The European Court of Justice (Luxembourg) interprets EU law. This should not be confused with the European Court of Human Rights (Strasbourg), which interprets the European Convention on Human Rights. Examiners frequently comment on the number of times the two bodies are muddled!

In what ways and why has the EEC/EU developed and expanded since 1957?

REVISED

- The key goal of the European Economic Community/European Union is European peace and 'ever closer union' between the peoples of Europe.
- As a result, the EEC/EU has steadily expanded its membership (see Table 8.2). In step with this process, European treaties have further advanced European integration. In this way the **widening** of the EEC/EU has taken place at the same time as the **deepening** of the relationship between its member states.
- Nation-states have joined the EEC/EU because it has enabled them to take advantage of the trading opportunities offered by the single market.
- Membership of the EEC/EU has led to democracy being entrenched in former authoritarian states, such as Spain, Portugal and Greece.
- Membership has also provided security for new democracies in eastern Europe. As members of the EU they are better protected from being pulled back into the Russian sphere of influence.
- The expansion of the EEC/EU has given its members much greater geostrategic influence when negotiating with powerful nation-states such as the United States, Russia and China.

Widening–deepening refers to the way in which the EU has expanded its membership while also deepening levels of integration between its member states. It can be complicated to achieve both because the wider the membership of the EU, the more difficult it is to integrate such increasingly diverse nation-states.

Federalism refers to a system of government in which power is shared between central and more regional layers of government. Both possess sovereign powers, which means that neither is subordinate to the other. The European Union is an example of a federal system of government because it has both supranational and intergovernmental institutions of governance.

Exam tip

Be careful how you use the term **federalism**. In the UK the term is often used to mean a unified European state. It is more properly used to refer to a sharing of power between different layers of government.

Table 8.2 The EEC/EU: membership and treaties

Membership	Treaties
1951 Establishment of the European Coal and Steel Community: France, West Germany, Italy, Belgium, the Netherlands, Luxembourg	The Treaty of Paris (1951), which created the European Coal and Steel Community, included supranational institutions. This demonstrates that from its beginning the European project was focused on challenging state sovereignty.
1957 Establishment of the European Economic Community: France, West Germany, Italy, Belgium, the Netherlands, Luxembourg	The Treaty of Rome (1957) established the EEC's guiding principle of 'ever closer union'. The founding members committed to the removal of tariffs on goods between them and the adoption of a common external tariff. The Treaty also established supranational institutions such as the Commission and the European Court of Justice, to be balanced by the intergovernmental Council.
1973 Demark, Ireland, the United Kingdom	
1981 Greece	

→

Membership	Treaties
1986 Spain and Portugal	The Single European Act (1986) extended the free market in goods to services, capital and people. It also increased qualified majority voting on the Council of Ministers, leading to a more integrated Europe.
1995 Austria, Finland, Sweden	The Maastricht Treaty (1992) dramatically advanced European integration by transforming the Community into a Union. It also established a common EU citizenship and set out plans for economic and monetary union (EMU) and a common foreign and security policy. However, Maastricht also recognised the principle of subsidiarity whereby the European Union should make decisions only if they are not better taken by nation-states. This safeguards the sovereign independence of its members.
2004 Estonia, Latvia, Lithuania, Slovenia, the Czech Republic, Poland, Hungary, Cyprus, Malta	The Amsterdam Treaty (1997) provided the EU with greater democratic legitimacy by giving more legislative influence to the Parliament. The Schengen principle of passport-free travel between member states was also included in the Treaty.
2007 Bulgaria/Romania	
2013 Croatia	As a result of its dramatic expansion since 2004, the aim of the Lisbon Treaty (2007) was to give the EU greater unity and coherence. The permanent position of EU Council President and EU High Commissioner for Foreign Affairs were created. The EU was also given a legal identity so that it can negotiate directly with nation-states through its own diplomatic service. Although qualified majority voting was further extended on the Council of Ministers, Article 50 provided a mechanism whereby nation-states may leave the European Union.

- In 2019, the following countries had all applied for membership of the European Union: Turkey, Iceland, Bosnia, Macedonia, Serbia, Montenegro, Albania. Kosovo had also applied, but not all EU states recognise its independence from Serbia.

Exam tip

Be careful not to confuse the EU President of the Council with the EU President of the Commission. The President of the Council represents EU leaders in foreign policy. The President of the Commission chairs the Commission as it formulates and implements EU policy.

Now test yourself

TESTED

5 Explain the functions of the main supranational bodies of the European Union.
6 Why was the Maastricht Treaty (1992) so significant in the development of a more united Europe?
7 In what ways did the Lisbon Treaty (2007) change the European Union?
8 In what ways can the European Union still be seen as an intergovernmental organisation?

Answers on p. 110

The EU's development towards economic and monetary union

REVISED

- Since its establishment, the EEC/EU has been committed to achieving 'ever closer union'.
- Maastricht (1992) is a key treaty because it established Economic and Monetary Union (EMU). EMU aims to create a more prosperous, stable and united European Union. It does this by coordinating the economic, fiscal and monetary policies of its member states.

- By 2019, 19 members of the European Union had accepted complete economic and monetary union. These member states comprise the Eurozone. Seven other EU states were working towards EMU, with only the UK and Denmark having secured opt-outs.
- All new members of the European Union are obliged to work towards full economic and monetary union.
- The financial crisis which began in 2007 strengthened the case for further economic and monetary union in order to help the EU withstand external economic threats. In 2012 the Fiscal Compact required EU states to balance their budgets and accelerated steps towards convergence. Only the UK and the Czech Republic opted out.
- As a result of the UK's decision to leave the EU, it is likely that the European Union will eventually achieve total economic and monetary union.
- If this occurs, the European Union will be significantly closer to becoming a full political union since all economic and monetary policy will be decided supranationally.

Debates about supranational versus intergovernmental approaches

REVISED

- Since its establishment in 1957, the EEC/EU has had to balance the competing claims of its supranational and intergovernmental institutions.
- Those who see the EU as primarily an intergovernmental organisation argue that it was established to serve the interests of its member states.
- The principle of subsidiarity (Maastricht Treaty, 1992), which states that decisions should be made by EU institutions only when they are not better made by the member states, supports an intergovernmental interpretation of the EU.
- The Lisbon Treaty (2007) also established the principle that member states may leave the EU (Article 50). This would not be the case if the EU was entirely supranational.
- However, supranationalists argue that ever since the Schuman Declaration, the goal of the European project has been full European unity. This is why all EEC/EU treaties have reduced the sovereign independence of member states.
- Only by becoming a distinct political entity will the EU be able to banish nationalism and so guarantee European peace. A united Europe will also be able to assert more global influence.
- President Macron of France has called for greater European unity as a way of defeating nationalism and giving the EU greater global influence so that it does not 'become a plaything of great powers'.
- Critics of this approach argue that the rise of populism and nationalism across Europe has been provoked by European integration moving too fast without the consent of the public. They claim that the vision of a supranational united Europe, far from defeating nationalism, has actually encouraged it.

The significance of the EU as an international body/global actor

REVISED

- The geostrategic power of the EEC/EU has developed as a result of its growing economic unity and strength. This means that it wields considerable influence as an economic superpower.

- The Maastricht Treaty (1992) established a common foreign and security policy, providing the EU with the means to coordinate a united position in international relations.
- The Lisbon Treaty (2007) provided the EU with a legal identity and created the permanent positions of President of the Council and High Commissioner for Foreign Affairs. As a result, the EU now has the authority and leadership positions to better represent itself in international relations.
- The EU can exert economic, political, structural, military and soft power influence. However, the extent to which it wields these powers effectively is controversial.
- Critics argue that the EU lacks world influence because its member states do not share a coherent global vision. Therefore, on important global issues it has been very difficult to achieve a coherent and consistent European perspective.
- The fact that the EU lacks military influence also means that it does not have a key element of hard power. As a result, its influence can be ignored when trying to resolve crises such as the Russian annexation of Crimea (2014) and the Syrian civil war (2011).

Global actor refers to a nation-state or an intergovernmental organisation such as the European Union which is able to wield significant influence in global relations.

Debate

Is the EU a significant global actor?

Yes	No
The economic strength of the EU provides it with powerful global influence.	Since foreign and defence policy is subject to the national veto it is difficult to establish a united European front on important global issues.
The EU has been able to negotiate as an equal partner with the United States over the Transatlantic Trade and Investment Partnership.	Member states have very different strategic objectives and diplomatic loyalties and so consensus is difficult to achieve.
In 2017, the EU and Japan established the largest free-trade zone in the world, representing a third of the world's gross domestic product.	As a result, the EU lacks a sufficient sense of identity to be able to present clear policy on pressing regional issues such as how to respond to the Libyan revolution (2011), the Russian annexation of Crimea (2014) and the civil war which broke out in Syria in 2011.
The EU has collectively fined Apple and Google for improper trade practices.	
As a major investor in the developing world, the EU is able to incorporate requirements for human rights protection and democracy in its trade deals. It has done this most notably with the Cotonou Agreement with 79 countries in the developing world.	There has been no EU intervention against Islamism in Syria, although member states like France and the UK have taken military action.
The economic advantages of joining the single market have encouraged peace in the Balkans as aspiring member states have had to commit to peace, democracy and human rights.	In spite of its economic influence, the EU has been unable to exert influence on China to improve its human rights record.
	Most EU countries are in NATO and so rely upon NATO for their immediate military protection.
In 2016, Turkey agreed to cooperate with the EU in tackling the migrant crisis in return for easier visa entry into the EU for Turkish citizens and an acceleration of Turkey's application for EU membership.	Although the European Union has its own rapid reaction force, it does not have its own nuclear deterrent or aircraft carriers. Realists argue that this significantly reduces the EU's capacity for global influence and outreach.
Tough EU sanctions encouraged Iran to agree to limits being put on its nuclear programme in 2015.	The EU only has observer status at the United Nations and does not have a seat on the Security Council.

→

Yes	No
In 2017, the EU imposed an arms embargo in Venezuela following disputed elections and the shooting of anti-government protestors. The growing structural power of the EU is demonstrated by the way in which the EU is represented on the WTO, the G7 and the G20. EU military forces have conducted several peacekeeping operations, including the Democratic Republic of the Congo, Macedonia, Bosnia and Kosovo. The EU also exerts considerable soft power influence. At UN climate change summits, such as Paris, it has provided global leadership by setting ambitious carbon-reduction targets. As the world's largest provider of overseas aid, the EU has considerable moral influence.	The EU's ability to promote liberal democratic values is being constrained by the rise of European nationalist/populist parties which question these values. The rise of the 'America first' ideology of President Trump has reduced the EU's global influence as it can no longer claim to be the United States' closest ally. In 2019, the EU unanimously rejected Israel's claim to sovereignty over the Golan Heights. However, Israel ignored the EU, knowing Israel had the support of the United States. The global influence of the EU is also likely to be reduced by the departure of the UK since it is one of the EU's biggest economies and has had such an assertive foreign and defence policy.

Now test yourself

TESTED

9 What have been the main reasons for the expansion of the EU?
10 What is Economic and Monetary Union (EMU) and why is it so significant in the development of the European Union?
11 In what ways does the EU wield global influence?
12 What factors stop the EU from wielding more global influence?

Answers on pp. 110–11

To what extent does regionalism address and resolve contemporary global issues?

REVISED

Conflict

- The European Union has contributed to a number of peacekeeping missions, including Kosovo, Bosnia and the Democratic Republic of the Congo.
- In spite of this the EU has had a minimal role in trying to resolve conflicts such as the Syrian civil war, ongoing conflict in Libya and tensions in Ukraine, even though these directly impact on EU security.
- African Union forces have been involved in peacekeeping operations in Burundi, Sudan, Democratic Republic of the Congo and Mali.
- However, the AU has failed to take the initiative in conflicts such as the disputed election in Ivory Coast (2010–2011) or the overthrow of President Omar al-Bashir in Sudan (2019).
- The Arab League has also failed to intervene in crises such as Syria and Libya.
- ASEAN has been especially criticised for ignoring the persecution of the Rohingya Muslims in Myanmar.

Poverty

- By encouraging trade liberalisation, regional organisations have usually been seen as reducing poverty.
- Among ASEAN members, GDP per capita increased by 63.2% between 2007 and 2015 as a result of more opportunities for trade.
- The African Union's New Partnership for Africa's Development is committed to combatting poverty by more closely integrating African economies.
- However, the EU's external tariff and the Common Agricultural Policy (CAP), which protects European farmers, have been criticised for not opening up the EU to goods from the developing world.
- The EU's unwillingness to open up its agricultural markets to competition from the developing world was one of the main reasons for the collapse of the Doha Round of WTO trade talks.
- A main criticism of NAFTA was that it encouraged poverty in the United States by facilitating the flow of manufacturing jobs to Mexico. Rural Mexico also saw an increase in poverty as jobs in agriculture were lost to huge American agri-businesses.

Human rights

- The EU is committed to upholding human rights. The EU Charter of Fundamental Rights protects the human rights of all EU citizens and residents. The Cotonou Agreement requires developing countries to advance human rights and democracy in order to gain access to EU markets.
- However, the EU has failed to pressurise China to improve its record on human rights.
- In 2019, at the EU's first summit with the Arab League at Sharm El-Sheikh, President Sisi of Egypt told EU Council President Donald Tusk, 'You are not going to lecture us about humanity . . . Respect our values and ethics as we do yours.'
- In 2012 ASEAN adopted a Human Rights Declaration. However, all ASEAN countries have been accused of human rights abuses.
- In 2019, ASEAN member Brunei introduced the death penalty for sexual relations between men. In spite of global condemnation, ASEAN did not raise objections since it is committed to not interfering in the internal legal affairs of its member states.
- Only five of the ten ASEAN states do not criminalise homosexuality.
- Members of the Arab League, especially Saudi Arabia and Egypt, have been accused of systematic human rights abuses.
- The African Union has been criticised for condoning the human rights abuses of dictators such as the ousted President of Sudan, Omar al-Bashir.

The environment

- The EU provides a global lead on climate change. It is committed to cutting member states' carbon emissions by 40% of 1990 levels by 2030 and aims to be carbon neutral by 2050.
- However, member states of regional organisations such as the African Union, ASEAN and the Arab League continue to set their own carbon targets.

Exam practice

Section A

1 Examine the main differences between economic and political regionalism. [12]
2 Examine why the EEC/EU has deepened and expanded since its establishment in 1957. [12]

Section C

3 Evaluate the extent to which the European Union has acted as a model for other regional organisations. [30]
4 Evaluate the extent to which all regional organisations equally challenge the sovereignty of their member states. [30]
5 Evaluate the extent to which regional organisations are effective in protecting human rights. [30]
6 Evaluate the extent to which the European Union is a significant global actor. [30]

Answers and quick quiz 8 online

ONLINE

Summary

You should now have an understanding of the following:

- the distinction between the various types of regionalism (economic, political and security)
- the ways in which regionalism is a response to globalisation
- the different reasons why the Arab League, the African Union, ASEAN and NAFTA were established
- the extent to which these regional organisations can claim to be successful
- why the EEC/EU might be seen as a unique example of regionalism
- the meaning and significance of intergovernmentalism and supranationalism
- the ways in which the EEC/EU has developed since its establishment in 1957
- to what extent the EU is a significant global actor.

Now test yourself answers

Chapter 1

1 Realists believe that nation-states are motivated by self-interest. This means that they seek to protect their sovereignty and advance their strategic interests.

2 Realists believe there is no authority greater than the nation-state to which nation-states are accountable.

3 'Global anarchy' does not mean that there is constant war and confusion, but it does mean that there is no ultimate authority which can compel nation-states to obey.

4 Realists believe that global politics is anarchic because there is no supranational authority capable of enforcing its authority on nation-states.

5 According to realism, nation-states should increase their defences in order to protect themselves. The problem is that this will encourage other nation-states to do the same, so creating dangerous and destabilising arms races. This is known as the security dilemma.

6 Realists believe that state sovereignty is inviolable and argue that the preservation of sovereignty is the highest goal of any nation-state. Issues of morality therefore are of no consequence in global politics.

7 Realists believe that nation-states have to survive in an anarchic and potentially hostile world. Therefore, the accumulation of greater power provides the best way of maintaining your sovereignty against the hostility of other nation-states.

8 According to both realism and traditional conservatism, human beings are motivated by the selfish desire for power. As a result, strong governments are needed to provide protection from the predatory instincts of others.

9 Liberals have a positive view of human nature. They therefore believe that it is possible for nation-states to work together in order to resolve collective dilemmas.

10 Institutions of global governance bring together nation-states and non-state actors to make collective decisions. Liberals favour this collective form of decision-making, which challenges state egoism.

11 Since liberals believe in the importance of our shared humanity, the global protection of human rights is of paramount significance.

12 According to the liberal democratic peace thesis, liberal democracies which trade together will not go to war with each other. Thus the expansion of democracy and free trade contributes to global peace and security.

Chapter 2

1 A nation-state possesses absolute sovereignty. This means that it has complete authority over everything that happens within its borders. Therefore no other authority has the legal right to interfere within the borders of a sovereign nation-state.

2 Economic globalisation refers to the spread of free-market/free-trade ideals. This is referred to as the Washington Consensus and has been encouraged by institutions of global governance such as the World Trade Organization, the International Monetary Fund and the World Bank.

3 Political globalisation is the growing cooperation of nation-states in institutions of global and regional governance such as the United Nations or the European Union.

4 Cultural globalisation is the development of one global culture. This is closely associated with consumerism and brand recognition of the same global brands, which creates a more homogenised world culture.

5 According to neoliberals, economic globalisation is the most effective way of increasing global wealth and pulling people out of poverty. However, according to world systems/dependency theory, economic globalisation floods the developing world with cheap products so it never escapes a state of neocolonial servitude.

6 Collective decisions are made in regional organisations such as the European Union. The United Nations provides a forum for collective decision-making on issues such as climate change and stopping the proliferation of weapons of mass destruction.

7 The cultural homogenisation associated with materialism and consumerism has led to a backlash against such 'bland' and 'soul-less' uniformity. This can be seen with the rise of identity politics associated with Russian nationalism or global Islamism.

8 Nation-states still determine the burden of taxation on their citizens. They also decide the nature and extent of the civil liberties that their citizens possess.

9 The UN World Summit (2005) agreed Responsibility to Protect. This established the important principle that the sovereignty of a nation-state is conditional upon it not abusing the human rights of its citizens. Its practical impact has been demonstrated by the lack of humanitarian intervention in the Syrian civil war in spite of the massive loss of life.

10 International courts and tribunals, including the European Court of Human Rights and the International Criminal Court, protect human rights. Their effectiveness is undermined by state sovereignty however.

11 The way in which economic globalisation has dramatically increased global trade has contributed to growing carbon emissions. However, political globalisation, by bringing nation-states together in intergovernmental institutions of global governance, provides opportunities to collectively address environmental problems.

12 The spread of a homogenous global culture based on consumerism and materialism has provoked an identity backlash, such as Islamism, which has increased global tensions.

Chapter 3

1 The UN Security Council is able to mandate military action, under Article 7 of the UN Charter, in order to respond to aggression and prevent conflict. In order for this to happen, however, no permanent member of the Security Council can veto action.

2 The UN Security Council can mandate military action and so has the key function in determining the UN's response to conflict and aggression. The General Assembly debates issues of global concern. Its resolutions are non-binding but contribute to a global dialogue between nation-states.

3 The membership of the UN Security Council does not reflect the current global distribution of power, and the veto power of the permanent five makes it difficult to decide on military action. However, deciding which new countries should join the permanent five would be contentious. If the veto power were removed, although decisions could be reached more quickly, it is possible that the great powers would withdraw their support for the United Nations.

4 There is a strong case that there should have been a collective response by the United Nations to the civil war in Syria. However, because Russia supports the Assad regime it has not been possible to achieve a consensus.

5 Although the International Court of Justice has resolved some disputes, these have relied upon nation-states being prepared to cooperate with the court and accept its judgments.

6 The United Nations Declaration of Human Rights provides a standard of human rights for nation-states to aspire to. The UN High Commissioner for Human Rights and the UN Human Rights Council also publicise examples of human rights abuse.

7 UN relief agencies provide a vital way of addressing poverty, especially in emergency situations. However, UN aid agencies have been criticised for overlapping jurisdictions and inefficiency.

8 The UN Framework Convention on Climate Change has provided an important way of bringing nation-states together in climate change conferences to achieve a united approach to the problem. However, the way in which nation-states still prioritise their economic interests makes it difficult to achieve greater progress.

Chapter 4

1 The IMF and the World Bank are committed to free-market principles of neoclassical development. The structural adjustment programmes which they require in return for loans require nation-states to adopt free-market reforms. Critics claim that this challenges the economic sovereignty of nation-states.

2 According to Immanuel Wallerstein's world systems theory, the spread of a global free market disadvantages developing countries because they become reliant on cheap exports from the developed world. They therefore become dependent on the developed world and so do not develop their own industrial base.

3 Critics claim that IMF/World Bank structural adjustment programmes have undermined developing countries' economies by opening them up to foreign competition too soon. These allegations have been made especially in regard to Sub-Saharan African countries. However, supporters claim that the success of Southeast Asian countries, as well as the high growth rates of developing countries such as Ethiopia, has been due to the adoption of free-market reforms.

4 The World Bank has been responsible for important development programmes involving infrastructure development and fighting infectious diseases such as AIDS and tuberculosis.

5 The World Trade Organization is committed to reducing trade barriers between member states in order to encourage global free trade. It also resolves trade disputes between member states. Doha, the most recent round of WTO trade talks, has been criticised for failing to achieve a consensus between the developed and the developing worlds on opening up markets.

6 The WTO has been criticised for failing to open up the markets of the developed world to products from the developing world. The WTO's lack of focus on workers' rights and environmental protection has also led to criticism.

7 The G7 aims to encourage dialogue and achieve consensus on important global issues between the world's most developed countries. The G7's declarations lack binding force and also require consensus.

8 The G20 brings together the world's most powerful economies in order to encourage dialogue and reach decisions. Like the G7 its decisions require consensus and its communiqués are non-binding on member states.

9 The Brandt Reports in the 1980s coined the term North/South divide to distinguish between the less developed and the developing worlds. It is a contested term because some of the world's fastest-growing economies are now in the Global South, leading to greater convergence between the Global North and the Global South.

10 Neocolonialism refers to the way in which developed (core) states sell cheap products to developing (peripheral) states so they do not industrially develop themselves and so remain dependent on the developed world.

11 The orthodox measure of development is in terms of economic growth and income. The alternative measure of development is in other ways, such as political freedom, sustainable development, workers' rights and gender equality.

12 The existence of large-scale corruption in the developing world has impacted on development by reducing incentives for business investment and reducing the effectiveness of international aid.

Chapter 5

1 The International Court of Justice (World Court) adjudicates disputes involving nation-states. The sovereignty of nation-states undermines its effectiveness and the Security Council is too divided to be relied upon to enforce its judgments in cases of non-compliance.

2 The International Criminal Court judges individuals accused of crimes against humanity, genocide and systematic human rights abuses. Many nation-states, including powerful countries like the United States, Russia and China, refuse to accept its jurisdiction and it lacks enforcement power.

3 The ICJ has resolved a number of disputes. However, these have generally not involved powerful nation-states.

4 Although the ICC has successfully prosecuted a number of cases, including the Congolese warlord Thomas Lubanga, the number of cases it has successfully prosecuted has been very small and all of them so far have involved Africa.

5 The UN tribunal for the former Yugoslavia has convicted a number of war criminals, most notably the high-profile Bosnian Serb war criminals Ratko Mladic and Radovan Karadzic.

6 The conviction of the Liberian president, Charles Taylor, has been significant because he is a former head of state. This has set an important precedent in international law that heads of state may be held accountable by international law.

7 The Rwandan tribunal established the principle that the media can be implicated in genocide and that rape can be used as an instrument of genocide. The tribunal for Sierra Leone established the principle that a head of state can be held accountable in international law.

8 'Victors' justice' means that those sitting in judgment represent the winning side or have a bias against the plaintiffs. The way in which the tribunal for the former Yugoslavia mainly convicted Serbs and Bosnian Serbs has led to claims of victors' justice. This is especially the case because allegations that NATO may have been responsible for war crimes during the 1999 Kosovo war were not examined by the tribunal.

9 Humanitarian interventions in Bosnia, Kosovo, East Timor, Sierra Leone and Ivory Coast are all generally seen as successful. All of them involved large-scale military involvement, achievable objectives and a considerable commitment to nation-building.

10 Interventions in Somalia and Libya have been much less successful. Somalia was already a failed state and US forces were unable to resolve the massive tribal and clan rivalries. In Libya, there was no attempt at nation-building following the overthrow of Colonel Gaddafi so Libya soon fell into anarchy.

11 Liberals argue that humanitarian intervention is justified because of our common humanity and an obligation to save strangers.

12 Realists criticise humanitarian intervention because of the way in which it can challenge

state sovereignty. According to realists, respecting sovereignty is the best way of protecting global peace and security. Humanitarian interventions, such as those in Somalia, have been criticised for not achieving their objectives. Humanitarian interventions have also been criticised for being used to justify the geostrategic interests of nation-states.

Chapter 6

1 The UNFCCC has been ratified by all member states of the United Nations. It recognises the importance of keeping global temperature increase as low as possible and coordinating a global response to the problem.

2 The IPCC brings together scientists from across the world. The data and analysis that it produces provide the United Nations with the most up-to-date and reliable information available when it debates the issue of climate change.

3 Shallow green ecology approaches the issue of climate change from a human-centred (anthropocentric) perspective. It seeks to minimise the impact of climate change on human beings without a radical change to the way we live our lives. According to deep green ecology, we must protect the planet not out of self-interest but out of reverence for it. Deep green ecology requires much more radical changes to minimise the impact of humans on the planet.

4 Sustainable development is development which provides for the needs of today without damaging the planet for future generations. The way in which governments and people generally make decisions based on immediate considerations of self-interest makes this difficult to achieve.

5 According to the tragedy of the commons, the commons became exhausted because individuals overgrazed it for their own material advantage and so it was ruined for everyone. The same principle applies today to how the resources of the planet are being exhausted.

6 Developing countries have been reluctant to share the same burden of cutting carbon emissions as those in the developed world because historically they have contributed less to carbon emissions. Developing countries have also preferred to carry on using coal to power industrialisation because it is such a cheap form of fuel. Developed countries have also measured carbon emissions by total output while developing countries have measured it per head, which because they are so populous makes their carbon emissions seem less than they are.

7 Since nation-states resent supranational limits being put on their carbon emissions, at Paris in 2015 the only way a treaty could be negotiated was if member states set their own targets. This demonstrates the ongoing significance of state sovereignty in limiting action on climate change.

8 The Trump administration withdrew from the Paris Treaty because it felt it was damaging the American economy. This clearly demonstrates the way in which the economic self-interest of nation-states makes it difficult to make progress on how to address climate change.

Chapter 7

1 Soft power enables its holders to achieve global influence through the persuasiveness of their world view. This is a risk-free way of gaining influence; however, it depends upon others being prepared to adopt that world view, so its effectiveness is uncertain. The use of hard power can compel obedience through the deployment of economic and military power. However, military and economic conflict can result in unpredictable, dangerous and costly outcomes.

2 India is an emerging power because it has very strong growth rates, is increasingly assertive in international relations and possesses a strong military with developing outreach.

3 The United States is a superpower because it can extend its influence anywhere in the world. Although the UK plays an influential role in global decision-making bodies such as the United Nations and NATO, it is not able to assert its influence globally because there are greater limitations to its military, economic and diplomatic outreach.

4 A superpower possesses such dominant economic, diplomatic and military outreach that it is able to unilaterally assert its influence anywhere in the world and at any time. A great power plays a significant role in global decision-making and will play a major role in its near abroad. It will not, however, be able to assert its influence globally without the need for allies.

5 Realists believe that bipolarity provides stability and equilibrium. They favour it over a multipolar distribution of power which is more fluid and may encourage risk-taking by nation-states.

6 A benign hegemon can act as a global policeman and other nation-states can bandwagon behind it. However, if a hegemon is viewed as being in decline, this can encourage emerging powers to challenge its authority. This creates an unstable situation known as the Thucydides Trap. Unipolarity has also been criticised because it can enable a hegemon to act in defiance of international law.

7 The United States possesses unrivalled military and diplomatic outreach and the US economy

is still the biggest in the world. The US military is still, by far, the biggest globally and the United States is the only power able to make its influence felt anywhere in the world.

8 The growing military self-confidence of Russia and China's growing economic and military power both make them seem a challenge to US hegemony. The size of the EU economy also makes it a potential competitor to the United States. However, the EU lacks the military influence and united foreign policy to pose a realistic challenge, and neither China nor Russia possesses the global military outreach of the United States.

9 According to the democratic peace thesis, democracies value the rights of their citizens and by engaging in free trade create the conditions for a more connected world. This minimises the risk of war. However, realists counter that *all* states seek power and prestige so this suggests that the form of government of a state is irrelevant.

10 This is controversial because it is such a subjective term and critics claim that it has been used by the United States to label countries which it sees as a threat to its own national interests. Some radical political theorists have labelled the United States a rogue state because of the way in which it can ignore international law in pursuit of its own interests.

11 Failed states threaten global peace and stability because when there is no effective form of central government then a failed state can become a haven for terrorists and criminal gangs. This happened to Afghanistan in the 1990s and, more recently, has happened in Libya.

12 The way in which Russia and Iran have taken the lead in intervening in the Syrian civil war suggests that emerging powers are becoming more assertive. China is expanding its global economic influence and is increasingly assertive in its near abroad. In contrast, the United States has not provided global leadership in crises such as the Libyan or Syrian civil wars. Realists believe that this creates a dangerous situation since emerging powers may now gamble on challenging US hegemony.

Chapter 8

1 NAFTA was established in order to facilitate and encourage trade between the United States, Canada and Mexico. The Trump administration renegotiated it because it believed that as a result of the agreement, the United States was losing too many manufacturing jobs to Mexico.

2 The African Union seeks to achieve greater economic and political unity within Africa. So far its attempts to reduce trade barriers between member states, establish a common currency and achieve a sense of political unity have achieved very little.

3 The lack of consensus within the Arab League over how to resolve civil war in Syria and the ongoing conflict in Yemen highlights the deep-seated divisions within the League.

4 ASEAN was established to encourage trade and cooperation within its member states and to act as an economic counterweight to China and Japan. Compared with the European Union, it has made relatively little progress towards creating its goal of a fully functioning single market.

5 The supranational bodies of the European Union exercise authority over the member states. They include the Commission, which acts as the government of the European Union, and the Parliament, which has a legislative and scrutinising function. The European Court of Justice interprets the meaning of European law and the European Central Bank sets a common interest rate for the member states of the Eurozone. The supranational elements of the European Council of Ministers have increased since more decisions are now made using qualified majority voting, reducing the number of occasions when nation-states can use the veto.

6 The Maastricht Treaty was so significant because it established the principle of European economic and monetary union. It also committed the European Union to a common foreign and defence policy and established a European citizenship. Significantly, the European Community was renamed the European Union.

7 The Lisbon Treaty advanced European unity by creating an elected European Union Council President and a European Union High Commissioner for Foreign Affairs. It also provided the EU with a legal identity so that it can negotiate with nation-states. However, Lisbon also recognised the principle of subsidiarity, which is that decisions should be made as close to European citizens as possible.

8 The European Union retains significant intergovernmental features because on the European Council of Ministers/European Council key decisions which define a nation-state, such as those involving defence, foreign policy and taxation, still require unanimity. This means that nation-states can still exercise the veto on issues such as foreign policy, defence, non-EU immigration and taxation.

9 The expansion of the EU has been due to a combination of ideological and economic factors. Its founders believe that European integration would encourage peace and stability within Europe. Nation-states have also joined the EU in